# CAUGHT UP IN TIME

Oral History Narratives of Appalachian Vietnam Veterans

by

## John Hennen

**FIRST EDITION**



AEGINA PRESS, Inc.
59 Oak Lane, Spring Valley
Huntington, West Virginia 25704

# Dedication

Dedicated to Roy L. Ramey, SP4, United States Army, killed in action in Vietnam, June 6, 1969, and to Justin, Derek, and Louis, with hope that their generation not have its own Vietnam.

# Table of Contents

# Introduction

There is no common denominator of experience for Vietnam veterans. Each one's reaction to the war is to a great extent inner-directed, even if he or she has found responsive listeners. Molded by their participation in a war which defies reduction to clear perceptions and irrefutable declarations, they have often been defined as much by their identity as Vietnam veterans as by their names and occupations. As participants in an individualized war, they are a heterogeneous body, partially segregated by when they were in Vietnam, what their duties and actions were, their own understanding of the war and their role in it, and the responses to which they have been exposed since their return.

Vietnam veterans are a significant minority group of a largely alienated generation. They are a minority bound as much by the postwar oppression they endured as a class as by the oppression they suffered as willing or unwilling warriors for an ambiguous, ignoble cause in Southeast Asia. Thus, Vietnam veterans in great numbers were doubly oppressed, as pawns in an unjust war and as tangible symbols of the destruction of America's claims to political and social magnanimity.

This history uses oral narratives and written sources to develop local and national perspectives on some of the conflicts faced by the soldiers who served in Vietnam. The focus of the work is on the experience of Appalachian Vietnam veterans, more specifically West Virginia veterans. The narratives reflect the broad experience and wide range of perception of those veterans. Those interviewed included veterans who are political or apolitical, emotionally damaged or emotionally stable, securely employed or out of work, physically mutilated or physically whole, angry or passive, cynical or hopeful. Interviewed from September, 1984 to June, 1986 for the Marshall University Oral History of Appalachia Project, the participants included one nurse, one physician, several counselors, two lawyers, one contractor, one clothier, two doctoral candidates in anthropology, two students, an artist, a prosthetist, a teacher, a fire inspector, one career Army officer, and two chronically unemployed. Some served in Vietnam at an early period of American involvement, the earliest being in an advisory capacity in 1962. Most served between 1966 and 1970, one in 1972. Some were volunteers, some were draftees. Only two went to Vietnam as officers. Some saw heavy combat, some saw very little. Two returned to Vietnam for non-combat roles, one to defend military prisoners in Long Binh jail, the other to work for a Catholic relief agency serving Vietnamese refugees from the war. Two participated in the

Phoenix program, a Central Intelligence Agency assassination program designed to eliminate the Viet Cong infrastructure (VCI) from the Vietnamese countryside. One, James (Bud) Jordan, applied for conscientious objector status on grounds of personal ethics, after his enlistment in the Army, when he developed strong objections to the war. Jordan's application was denied, and he spent a year in prison at Fort Leavenworth when he refused to train with a weapon.

The theme of this work is conflict, and each interrelated chapter develops that theme. The conflicts include not only those inherent to combat, but those between ideology and political reality, Vietnam veterans and public institutions, veterans and their non-veteran peers, and those conflicts which have developed among Vietnam veterans themselves. The work outlines the historical economic development of West Virginia, and suggests how that development has influenced the participation of West Virginians in the armed forces and in combat. It recounts the ideological foundation of America's post-World War II political structure, how ideology affected young Appalachians' concept of national service, and how that concept was challenged by Vietnam and its aftermath. Part of the work documents the neglect of Vietnam veterans by older veterans and the American public, and the consequent national and local development of a Vietnam veterans political lobby. Included in that chapter are observations about the dissonance within the Vietnam veterans lobby brought about by the divisiveness of the war and veterans' disparate outlooks on their role in Vietnam and in history. Finally, the book includes analyses of Vietnam veterans within the framework of public education in West Virginia and resurgent American nationalism.

The history of the Vietnam war and its American soldiers reveals that economic and cultural inequities in the United States played major roles in determining which young men were sent into combat. Those inequities have traditionally been acute in much of Appalachia and the state of West Virginia. But the poor and the poorly educated throughout America carried more than their share of the burdens of the war in Vietnam and the turmoil of its aftermath. This volume focuses on the personal conflict of soldiers from one depressed area, but young men from Silvis, Illinois, or Bellingham, Washington, or Laurinburg, North Carolina, or New York City were subject to many of the same injustices as those from Cabin Creek, West Virginia. Documenting the responses of Appalachian Vietnam veterans to the trauma of their generation is important to the study of regional history. It is also important to the greater process of insuring that a future generation, from whatever region, does not endure another such trauma.

Without the guidance and support of many people, this volume would be no more than a gleam in the eye of a professional dishwasher. They offered advice, criticism, fellowship, and the benefits of their learning and experience. With sincere appreciation, thank you to Dr. David Woodward, Dr. William Palmer, and the remainder of the history faculty at Marshall University for dedication to the scholarship and welfare of their students, and for stoic good spirit in a world which undervalues their craft. Thanks to Juanita Harold and Yvonne Tumblin for their good cheer and workmanship, and to Katie Johnson, Jessica Elza, Todd Sykes, Carla Thompson, and Vina Hutchinson for transcribing tapes. The Marshall Graduate School generously sponsored my research with grants in 1985 and 1986. Elinore and Nancy Taylor sponsored publication. My comrades in *Marshall Action for Peaceful Solutions* (MAPS), especially David McGee, Janet Dooley, Laurie McKeown, Joe Eckhart, and Melissa Blagg, who faithfully apply the lessons of education where they are most vital, have helped me struggle toward a richer perspective on who we are, why we are here, and what we must do.

It was my privilege at Marshall to work closely with Dr. Frances Hensley, from whom I received consistent support and reasoned counsel from the beginning of my graduate work to the conclusion of my research. Sally Keaton of the Oral History of Appalachia Project has given freely of her gentle nature, infinite patience, and uncanny abilities to anyone who needed guidance. Her contributions to oral history in West Virginia are immeasurable.

Were it not for the critical honesty and constant faith of my colleagues in the graduate history program, it is likely that doubt and frustration during various and sundry crises would have sent me hightailing it for the Blue Ridge. To Todd Adkins, Herschel Cohen, Jim Deeter, Craig Houston, Alvie Qualls, Bruce and Angie Thompson, and my good friend Montserrat Miller Chambers, you have my good will and affection. Thank you to my friends Stuart, Jacqueline, and Elliot Downs, who have always given me a home, and to Mike Klein and the great Jim Smythers, who have always given me companionship and a soapbox. My sincere appreciation goes to those who agreed to share their thoughts and souls with the Vietnam Veterans Oral History Project. All of their names are listed elsewhere, but thank you particularly to Perry Campbell, Dave Evans, Bill Fox, Glen Hager, Doug Johnson, Robert Muller, Roger Sanford,

Ernestine Thornton, John Williams, Bud Jordan, and Gig Hobble. We can only imagine the sacrifices they and their comrades have made, or the impact their lives have on all of us.

For two years it was my great fortune to work and study under the direction of Dr. Robert Sawrey for the Oral History of Appalachia Project. Dr. Sawrey was always available to offer criticism, suggestions, assistance, and reinforcement. He displayed patience and an open mind both in class and private consultation, yet was sustained by controlled rage at arrogance, indifference, and injustice. He proved to be a valued and insightful teacher, and a trusted friend. My association with the Vietnam veterans project was a meaningful learning experience, and I am proud to have been a part of it.

Finally, thanks to my family, whose faith and love have helped guide me through various careers; especially to my father, who has passively instilled in me a passion for our language and simple living, and to the memory of my mother, who fought to cultivate in her children and grandchildren compassionate hearts and a love for open inquiry.

With their drums and guns and guns and drums, Huroo! Huroo!
With their drums and guns and guns and drums, Huroo! Huroo!
With their drums and guns and guns and drums,
the enemy nearly slew ye,
My darlin', dear, you look so queer,
Johnny I hardly knew ye.

Where are the legs with which you run? Huroo! Huroo!
Where are the legs with which you run? Huroo! Huroo!
Where are the legs with which you run,
when first you went to carry a gun?
Indeed, your dancin' days are done,
Johnny I hardly knew ye.

-Irish Ballad

# Ain't No Reason to Wonder Why:
# Young Appalachians, National Service,
# and Going to Vietnam

Few young Americans were familiar with the geopolitical, economic, and cultural factors which contributed to American involvement in the war in Vietnam. Believing in the goodness and morality of American domestic and foreign policy, draft-age men in the early to mid-1960s, particularly those from rural, tradition-bound areas, regarded military training as part of society's natural order. This chapter investigates factors which influenced young Americans, particularly West Virginians, to accept military training and the disillusionment which began to surface in many soldiers under fire, soldiers who were confronted with radical challenges to their beliefs about national service and the conduct of war. The conflicts between idealistic perceptions of fighting and realities of combat in a confusing war set the stage for political and emotional transformations in Americans who fought in Vietnam. Different steps in such transformations, when one's cherished accepted beliefs collided with one's own country and people, form the foundation for subsequent chapters.

The Gulf of Tonkin resolution, signifying Congressional approval of the escalation of American military involvement in the Vietnamese conflict, was passed on August 4, 1964. Between that date and March 28, 1973, when the last American troops left Vietnam, over twenty-six million American men became eligible for draft registration.[1] Nationally, men from predominantly rural states were twice as likely to be sent to Vietnam as those from highly urban states.[2] Historically, young Appalachians have been disproportionately represented in the military and in combat situations. During World War I, the state of West Virginia led the nation in the percentage of draft registrants called for induction who qualified for that distinction. Nearly nine hundred West Virginia soldiers died in combat in the Korean War. Seven hundred-eleven West Virginians, or 85 for every 100,000 males in the state, were killed in Vietnam, more per capita than any other state.[3] A high percentage of young West Virginia men volunteered for service in Vietnam, a war in which a sizable majority of those in combat were enlistees.[4]

In the years after World War II and the Korean War, young American men grew up facing the possibility of military service. Some dreaded the possibility, some were indifferent, and some eagerly anticipated military service as a source of excitement or a potentially valuable career decision. Perhaps, some believed, the military would offer them a chance to demonstrate their manhood, serve their country, and live an adventure before settling into conventional adulthood.[5] For many West Virginians, the military appeared to offer better options and training than those available for young adults who lived in a region of limited vocational and educational opportunities. In Central Appalachia, for instance, which includes the southern counties of West Virginia, 35% of the families lived below the federal poverty level in 1970 and 72% of the adult population had less than a high school education. Historically, an important factor causing Appalachians to enter the service was dissatisfaction with a monotonous existence. During times of national crisis, as word of the outside world reached the coalfields, young men sought in the Army the adventure which they had never seen. Military service afforded a relatively easy emotional transition from a family-oriented environment, substituting military authority for familial. Many rural boys, in addition, were "pre-trained" to be good soldiers, having had experience in hunting and woodsmanship. The military, realizing these factors, has traditionally directed Appalachians into combat roles.[6]

Perhaps the most salient factor of the economic legacy of Appalachia is the lack of job opportunities and upward mobility. Economic factors should not be underestimated in examining the attractiveness of military options for Appalachian men. Historically lacking a diversified economy, much of the land and resources in the state of West Virginia, for instance, has been owned and controlled for generations by absentee landlords. Shortly after the end of the Civil War, northeastern speculators embarked on an accelerated economic penetration of the Appalachian south. Geologists reported massive beds of bituminous coal under the forests. Coal, oil, and natural gas deposits, as well as vast tracts of land, were bought and exploited by outside investors with no cultural ties to the region. Corporate agents bought up the forest land at cheap rates and later took charge of the region's railroads, mines, furnaces and financial institutions. Some corporations were organized solely for the purpose of speculating in timber and mineral reserves, and virgin land passed from the hands of Appalachians, to whom a few hundred dollars was a substantial fortune, into the hands of absentee entrepreneurs, to whom a few hundred dollars was a night at the opera. To industrialists who opened mines, built railroads, and extracted the area's resources, the Appalachian population became a ready source of cheap labor, and the ownership of land and resources formed the basis of the distribution of wealth and power in Appalachia. The economy over which northeastern capital presided became one of "branch plants, branch banks, captive mines, and [company] stores." In West Virginia, the creation of a new state almost wholly subject to the social impact of the coal industry resulted in a "phenomenon best described as a colonial economy."[7]

Historian John A. Williams wrote that the history of the state of West Virginia illustrates a persistent economic reality, an antithesis "that is nearly always found between mountainous terrain and the economic uses of modern urban industrial society." Appalachians, said Williams, stood apart from the main currents of American industrial development, and whether or not mountaineers were always free (an allusion to the West Virginia state motto), they were almost always poor. Caught in the cycles of boom and bust inherent to a one-industry economy, a large percentage of the labor force in West Virginia has never enjoyed any degree of consistent economic security. Coal, said Williams, has been a curse on the land above it and the people who mined it. The coal industry, by its exploitation of workers and nature, and its "seemingly endless" series of disasters, has "brought grief and hardship to all but a small proportion of the people whose lives it has touched." The issue of West Virginia resources was not merely ownership but the extent to which the use of the state's resources were governed by the needs of the people and localities of the state. For example, although McDowell County in southern West Virginia produced more coal than any other county in the nation in 1970, the fact that two-thirds of that coal was owned by six out-of-state companies assured that the primary benefits of production left the region. Along with Kentucky and parts of Virginia, West Virginia developed as a "corporate fiefdom," providing enormous economic benefits to the rest of the nation while a deepening crisis of poverty and depression emerged in the hills. Absentee ownership, with its consequent neglect of the indigenous population, continues in West Virginia, with approximately two-thirds of the privately owned land held in absentia. Appalachia's huge mineral fields have remained in economic and political bondage.[8]

Parallels to the colonial nature of Appalachia's heritage abound in American ghettos and barrios, leading to strong indictments of class as a factor determining which Americans fought in Vietnam. Sociologist Robert Blauner described inner-city black ghettos in terms identical to Appalachian hollows when he wrote that the ghetto community could best be described as analogous to a powerless colony, wherein indigenous leaders were dependent on an outside political power structure and the economy was dominated by absentee ownership. Ironically, small independent coal operators in Appalachia often developed a negative evaluation of their own people and assumed even more rigid political and economic ideologies than the absentee owners themselves. Small operators, dependent on the outside corporations for leases, capital, and sales and transportation facilities, generally reflected the interests of the absentees. As a result, local economic and political power structures came under the influence of "native colonizers," speaking for the system which "kept the niggers down."[9]

The soldiers who fought and died in Vietnam were primarily the same men who "get left behind in schools, jobs, and other forms of social competition. Few of the nation's elite had sons or knew others who did any fighting."[10] When black soldiers accounted for a shocking 24% of all Army combat deaths in 1965, the Department of Defense took steps to reduce the proportion of minorities in combat situations. Despite the department's actions, social and economic inequities continued to play a major role in the profile of American combat troops. Poorly educated low-income blacks and whites did a "vastly disproportionate" share of the fighting. Those from economically disadvantaged backgrounds, such as rural and small town Appalachians, were two times as likely as their middle and high income peers to serve in the armed forces and fight in Vietnam.[11]

Given the heritage of economic exploitation in the state of West Virginia, one could reasonably assume that the predominance of West Virginia soldiers exposed to combat situations was an extension of that exploitation. The draft and the direction of soldiers into combat based on class and educational factors were functions of what Lawrence M. Baskir and William A. Strauss called a "Darwinian social policy," protecting those who had access to an elaborate structure of deferments, exemptions, and non-combat military alternatives. The draft rewarded those young men who learned to manipulate the selective service system, primarily young college men with access to draft counseling on the campuses. This manipulative process, biased in favor of the middle and upper classes, led to a common assessment of those who were drafted or enlisted as "suckers."[12]

Psychologist Kai Erikson traced elements of ruralism, specifically isolation, which support explanations of the special adaptability of Appalachian soldiers to the particular combat situations which were prevalent in Vietnam. These situations included rugged terrain, individual action within small patrols, and a demand for quick, seemingly instinctive responses. Rural life, wrote Erikson, bred an independence of thought and expression, an independence "profoundly reinforced by the conditions of life prevailing there." The harsh realities of poverty and isolation encouraged strong individualism which, while serving the Appalachian soldier well in the field, could and often did obstruct traditional lines of military discipline and later affected the Appalachian veterans' relationship with government bureaucracies. The mountain lifestyle highlighted the immediacy of experience, a resort to action as opposed to reflection, and a respect for feeling and sensation. Indeed, the mountains separated people into isolated hollows and impoverished company towns where they had "little choice but to rely on their own individual resources."[13]

Many West Virginia veterans seemed to confirm Erikson's thesis about Appalachians' adaptability to harsh physical realities by adjusting well to difficult conditions in the Vietnamese jungles and countryside. One of these was Randy Bowles, a Kanawha Valley native who was working as a maintenance mechanic in a Charleston laundry before he was sent to Vietnam in 1970. Bowles recalled that he had a particular talent for "walking point," or leading patrols through the undergrowth of Vietnamese jungles. Walking point, said Bowles, was the worst job one could have in combat; soldiers made every effort to avoid the duty "because they felt like they'd get blowed [sic] away first." Bowles insisted on cutting his own trails when he walked point in order to minimize the chances of tripping one of the booby-trapped mines which dotted existing jungle trails. Bowles alternated walking point with a Mexican-American soldier, and on occasion encountered criticism from members of his patrol upset at being off the trail:

> Guys would get mad at us and we would say "well, here. You cut point. We'll go to the end of the line and you can have all this [booby-trap danger] done to you." No matter how big they was, they understood that we knew what we was sayin'. We done it for three months and-a-half, and never run into any contact as far as ambush, or firefight or anything like that.[14]

Regardless of his acumen at walking point, however, Bowles's background and military training had ill-prepared him for the emotional challenges of Southeast Asia. He and his comrades functioned in a surreal environment in Vietnam, an environment which contradicted much of what they had known and accepted before. Patriotism, family tradition, economic hardship, boredom, and resignation to the inevitability of military service all contributed to the presence of Appalachians in Vietnam. There are approximately 30,000 Vietnam veterans in the state of West Virginia, and each one has his or her own theories, explanations, and memories of that most divisive, convulsive period in American history, the Vietnam era. Most are proud to have served their country, but they also have serious, often bitter, questions about the conduct of the war, the ambiguities of the American mission in Vietnam, and the painful legacies of that time which have intruded on their lives, their families, their careers, and their health. "We fought one war over there," recalled a Cabin Creek veteran, "but Vietnam veterans had to be ready to fight all over again when they got home."[15]

Bill Fox came from a relatively comfortable economic background, but his route to Vietnam was otherwise typical. Fox graduated from Huntington High School in June, 1966, and after flunking out of college in North Carolina, returned to Huntington in the winter of 1967 to live with his parents. He got a job in a Huntington pizza parlor. Fox, as a non-student facing the possibility of being drafted at any time, decided to volunteer for the draft. Restless at the prospect of remaining in his parents' home and uncertain about his suitability for college (he later earned a master's degree in counseling at Marshall University), Fox was nineteen and "wanted to get on with my life." He recalled the summer day in 1967 when he decided to volunteer:

> It was in July, I remember when a bunch of us boys were driving down here on 4th Avenue. All of a sudden I just said "well, I think I am going to do it" and I hollered out in the car, "who wants to go in the army with me?" And this one guy, Don Tipton, [said] "I'll go." It kind of shocked me . . . . I had this little pipedream in my head that I thought all five of us would go, like in the movies. But there was only two of us stupid enough.[16]

James Hill of Charleston, West Virginia enlisted in the Army in 1956. Joining the service was "the thing to do back in those days, it was just proper for a young man to go into the military." Hill, who was seventeen when he first enlisted, reenlisted shortly after his 1962 discharge, while living in Houston, Texas. "A lot of my friends were Cuban refugees," Hill remembered. When the Cuban missile crisis developed, "I decided I'd go down and kick Castro's ass." Hill, disappointed when "Castro and Khruschev backed down," feared he was destined to years of regular army routine. "But a guy named Ho Chi Minh started something in Vietnam so my three years was taken up." Hill served the first of three tours in Vietnam in 1963.[17]

Especially during the early years of America's involvement in Vietnam, the sense of national obligation mentioned by James Hill motivated many of those who volunteered to serve in Vietnam. Harry Beam enlisted in 1963 and became a career Army man, serving as the commander of the Reserve Officer Training Corps at Marshall University from 1984-86. Beam grew up in a Pennsylvania steel town, surrounded by a military tradition, a tradition reinforced by Beam's consciousness of his country being involved in military actions from his earliest memory. America was at war for the first five years of his life (1940-45), and when Beam was ten years old the North Koreans invaded South Korea:

> That had a very marked impression on me as a kid. As a matter of fact as a ten-year old kid I was the one who informed the family after hearing the news [of the Korean invasion] on the radio . . . . What I'm really saying is I've always had an interest in the military.[18]

Ernestine Thornton, born and raised in Wyoming County, West Virginia, joined the Army to further her career. The daughter of a coalminer who later became a mine owner himself, Thornton graduated from high school in 1959, then entered nursing school in Roanoke, Virginia. Upon completion of her program, Thornton worked as a nurse in Welch, West Virginia, and was anxious after two years there to expand her horizons. She was aware of "rumblings and rumors of war in Indochina," and began to consider a military career. Strongly influenced by the confident idealism of the presidency of John F. Kennedy, the "call to young people, [as] I think most people my age were, I finally made up my mind and entered the Army."[19]

Roger Sanford was raised in the west end of Huntington, West Virginia, graduating from Huntington High School in June, 1965. Sanford enrolled at Marshall University for over two years, but left school in 1968. Shortly thereafter, he received his draft notice. "Deep down inside I feel that I honestly wanted to go into the service, for adventure," Sanford recalled. "I think a lot of people from Appalachia were going to go there [Vietnam] for patriotism, some for adventure, some were unemployed. Nonetheless, I reported for induction." Sanford's father, who had served in the 66th Infantry Division in World War II, was so opposed to American military involvement in Vietnam that he attempted to substitute for his son when they arrived at the Armed Forces Examining and Entrance Station in Ashland, Kentucky, for Roger Sanford's physical. "[He] tried to take my place. He said he didn't want me to go, said the war was crazy, it made no sense. They said [to Sanford's father], you know, 'you can't do that'."[20]

Rick Richards of Charleston, West Virginia, came from a military background. Raised on military bases, Richards "thought in military terms all my life. I thought going to Vietnam would be a way to glory, a way to prove myself as a man."[21]

Dave Evans, a native of Cabin Creek, West Virginia, joined the United States Marine Corps at age sixteen, lying about his age on the enlistment forms. Evans, a miner's son, "went in thinking I was going to fight for democracy." He was "a poor kid, looking for a career, a way out of the coal mines." Evans found his career, as director of prosthetics for Medical Aid for El Salvador, a California based organization, which treats war victims. He designs and manufactures artificial limbs, a vocation in which he has a natural interest, having lost both legs below the knees near Chu Lai on December 4, 1970. "I went from being a kid in boot camp at sixteen to a squad leader at seventeen," said Evans, "then to a retired Marine Corps sergeant at nineteen going on forty."[22]

Doug Johnson of Huntington saw the military as a means to learn career skills, and remembered having little awareness of the specifics of the widening Vietnam war when he enlisted in the Marines in November, 1963. The Marine recruiter, Johnson recalled, "said nothing about Vietnam." The recruiter was, however, "a real square guy," telling Johnson that he might or might not actually be involved in combat while in the service, but that his basic job "will be to learn how to kill people." Johnson reasoned that he was not doing anything constructive with his life, having dropped out of Marshall University, and that perhaps "I can get a job or a career, along with this business of learning how to kill people. I was intrigued by that, because I wasn't a particularly violent type person at all."[23]

Although some Vietnam veterans, such as Harry Beam, had a somewhat sophisticated perspective on the political and historical background of the Vietnamese conflict before their personal involvement, most had little or no idea what their role was to be or the nature of the combat they were to face. "We were just kids," a Lewisburg veteran remembered. "I was nineteen. We were just kids. We really didn't know what the hell was going on. But we learned real fast."[24] For many, the magnitude of what they were about to experience, contrasted with what they had known before, began to intrude on them as they flew to Vietnam. For others, the conflict between previous reality and the new truth of Vietnam was delayed. Bill Fox was a radio operator at Ban Me Thuot, near the Vietnam/Cambodia border. Today he has definite opinions about the Vietnam war and his role in it. When he was shipped to Vietnam, however, he did not have any particular attitudes about his mission.

> And we flew. We just took off. It was so bizarre. I mean you see movies about people going off to war and there's parades and bands . . . . I mean there was nobody there. It was just routine, it was like cattle to the slaughter. There was no family, no waving goodbye, no sweetheart, stuff like that. We were just like a bunch of dumb cattle.[25]

Some of the troops on his flight were nervous, said Fox. "Some guys didn't give a shit and some guys were looking forward to it." Fox's reasoning was that the Army was using him and Vietnam was where it figured he was needed. "I'd been to Fort Knox, I'd been to Fort Benning, now I was gonna' go to Fort Vietnam." Fox began to understand the gravity of his situation upon receiving his orders at Cam Ranh Bay, the massive American transportation and deployment compound near Dalat on the South china Sea. Fox's assignment to Ban Me Thuot sent him to one of the "hotspots" in that section of Vietnam, an area which consistently received heavy mortar and rocket fire at night. "It finally dawned on me that I was in a place where people were shooting at each other. And there were people out there that wanted me dead."[26]

Fox's introduction to Southeast Asia was common for other Appalachians. A Virginia veteran had a parallel awakening shortly after his arrival in Vietnam. Al Van Dyke had "no idea what it was gonna' be like. None of that stuff was real, I didn't know what to expect." Van Dyke had never known anyone who had been to Vietnam when he was sent there in June, 1968:

> Even when I was in Vietnam the whole business of the war wasn't real until one night. I was walking up a path to go to a makeshift shelter that I lived in, [and] the dust started kicking up in front of me. And I thought that was pretty odd. Turned out it was somebody shootin' at me. That was the first time I thought, "hmm. This is something different." I thought, "This guy is personally

tryin' to kill me." And that's when I realized there was a war goin' on.[27]

Roger Sanford experienced a foreshadowing of the emotional conflict he faced in Vietnam as he prepared to leave Huntington. It was a difficult departure. "Just a few short months ago I was a kid on the street, going to Marshall University." Being only twenty years old and flying for the first time was "traumatic enough," Sanford recalled, "especially out of this [Tri-State] airport." As he awaited a connecting flight in Chicago for San Francisco, Sanford was struck by his first exposure to a small group of American combat veterans, returning from Vietnam and disbursing for their individual flights home. "You could see by their decorations and their patches and I guess the glaze in their eyes," said Sanford, "that they'd been somewhere that I hadn't been before. They'd seen a movie that I hadn't seen." He also noticed the looks on the faces of the stewardesses on his flight from San Francisco to Southeast Asia, "sad in a way. They probably made this run about once a week." Upon his arrival at the Bien Hoa airfield near Saigon, Sanford saw further evidence that he was entering a new world when he witnessed the personal belongings of a recently killed American soldier being poured onto the tarmac from a duffel bag. "They just load your stuff up and they take it there [and dump it]. That right there," said Sanford, "got people thinking 'what in the world?' I [had] a feeling that we're on a big roundup of cattle and that we're just starting before we get to the slaughteryards."[28]
The recollections of Appalachian Vietnam veterans are replete with a sense of resignation to one's fate and a simultaneous, passionate desire to avoid that fate. Appalachians, as a people whose cultural inheritance is marked by lack of personal control over their land and future, have often been characterized as possessing a pervasive fatalism or passive acceptance of one's condition. Sociologists have attributed fatalism in Appalachians to an unyieldingly harsh physical and economic environment, leading to the erosion of one's confidence in his/her ability to control his/her life. This erosion led to a "fatalistic attitude, which allowed [the Appalachian] to live without the guilty feeling that he himself was to blame for his lot." Fatalism in turn fostered passive resignation, and acceptance of undesirable conditions became a cultural trait.[29] Given the surreal situation of American combat soldiers in Vietnam, fatalism might seem a logical response. Yet, woven throughout the narrative of many Appalachian veterans, acceptance of one's fate is tempered with a stubborn determination to overcome that

fate and turn it to one's advantage.

For example, under heavy fire his first day in the field in Vietnam, Harry Beam entertained serious doubts as to whether he would survive his one year tour of duty. "This is my introduction," he thought. "This is the way it really must be." By the end of the first week, Beam had decided that he probably would not return home alive. "Even to this day, I'm sort of a fatalist in a way. I have a tendency to say 'when my time is up, it's up. It's not going to matter whether I'm on the battlefield or laying in bed." Beam believed his resignation to some extent allowed him to perform his combat duties more easily, somehow comforted by the absolute knowledge that he was going to die. About thirty days before he was to return home, however, "it occurred to me . . . that I really had a shot at getting home, and I was a lot more careful, and I stopped doing some things that were 'chivalrous'."[30] Some veterans have transformed passive acceptance of fate into positive activism, indicating that the fatalism often ascribed to Appalachians, rather than being a reflection of apathy, may in fact be an adaptive technique of the powerless. The crucible of Vietnam led some veterans to conclude that poverty and the Appalachian heritage of exploitation were not unique to the hollows and mining towns but raised questions about the politics of poverty in general. For some veterans, their Vietnam experience compelled them to reassess the power realities in America which sent them to the jungles. Dave Evans, a politically active advocate for veterans' rights and an outspoken critic of America's military involvement in Vietnam and Central America, attributed many veterans' political awakening to a belief that

> . . . we're not afraid to die 'cause we figure we're living on borrowed time anyway. Most of the people who have been [in combat] have this syndrome of living on borrowed time. That's the way I feel; I mean, I was so close to being fucking killed fourteen years ago that anything I do today is a bonus for me. In any stretch of the imagination I shouldn't be here today. I should be up on the fucking wall looking out at the monument today. [Evans was speaking of the "Three Soldiers" statue near the Vietnam Veterans Memorial wall in Washington.] I got about four people in my squad, five, they're on that damn wall looking out at the new monument. So anything I do to better the life of Vietnam vets is a plus for me. I've done something with my life.[31]

Rick Richards, former legislative coordinator of the West Virginia State Council of the Vietnam Veterans of America, expanded on the theme of soldiers under fire refusing to accept certain death. "Once you got out in the field," he explained, "your goal change[ed] from saving America for democracy to living through that year." Ambivalent about the purpose of their mission, unsure about the competence of civilian and/or military policymakers, confused and angry about the lack of popular support in the United States, and under constant stress in a war of ambushes, booby-traps, and unknown enemies, American combat soldiers lived for DEROS, the Date of Expected Return from Overseas. DEROS was the military's attempt to deflect or avoid problems associated with psychological breakdown under extended combat situations. Some long-range consequences of the DEROS idea will be addressed subsequently; it should be noted, however, that DEROS became a personalized, individual goal for each combatant, often at the expense of morale and the "integrity of the unit" which had helped sustain troops in more conventional combat situations. The immediate significance of DEROS, given that all military personnel were aware upon leaving the United States precisely when they would ride the "freedom bird" home, was that it held before each soldier an exit from the war aside from physical or psychological trauma or desertion. Hence, although the long-term psychological implications of DEROS have since become evident, the combat soldier typically indulged in a "DEROS fantasy," looking toward the great day of his release from all of the problems associated with the war. Survival became the overarching goal of the American combat soldier in Vietnam.[32]

Living through the year joined pervasive fear as the constants in the existence of most soldiers. Although some combatants thrived under the new realities of Vietnam, most shared with a West Huntington veteran an unsuitability to the "constant movement, constant danger. When I got over there and started coming under enemy fire [and] started seeing [physical] trauma and a lot of indescribable things, [my main goal] was survival. Three-hundred and sixty-five days." He volunteered for any sort of undesirable duty to avoid going out in the field, tasks such as burning oil drums of human excrement, identifying bodies, and stuffing body bags. "I just tried to utilize every day," he said. "Every day you gotta' figure out 'what am I gonna' do? If things get too bad, then I'll go on R[est] and R[ecreation] and not come back.' People did that, you know."[33]

The emotional shock of combat intensified in the troops as they began to question their purpose in Vietnam. American morale was severely damaged by the massive North Vietnamese and Viet Cong Tet offensive early in 1968, an offensive the magnitude of which troops in the field and Americans at home believed could not happen given the alleged depletion of enemy forces. As the military multiplied desperate tactical measures in the Vietnamese countryside, such as free-fire zones, carpet bombing, search and destroy operations, and assassination of suspected Viet Cong operatives, the conscience and emotional tolerance of American combat soldiers were tested. Many experienced the beginning of alienation from the institutions in which they had faith. One such veteran was Randy Bowles, who remembered a trip to a field hospital in Chu Lai, where he was to be treated for ringworm and jungle rot. A company from his battalion had run into a field of land mines, been cut up badly, and was being treated in the same hospital. Bowles entertained thoughts of desertion, afraid that his own company would meet a similar fate:

> These guys was messed up so bad. The morale with my company, by all this happenin', the guys was ready to desert, but they wouldn't do it. But these feelings went through every man's mind. They went through mine. In fact, I told my sergeant that I wasn't going to go out in the field, and he told me, "Who do you think you are? You think you're better than any of us?" I said, "No, they got the right to refuse to go into the field like I do."[34]

Shortly before his tour ended, Bowles survived a mortar attack in which most of his company were wiped out.

Doug Johnson of Huntington, who went on patrols with several different units as a weapons repair specialist on loan from the First Battalion, Third Marines, was assigned to the Ninth Marines for a short time. The Ninth, said Johnson, had "one of the highest attrition rates in Vietnam," due partly to "incompetent officers . . . . They'd screwed up and [mutilated] a bunch of these VC they'd found," said Johnson, "and after that they had a 'ghost battalion' [of Viet Cong] on their ass wherever they'd put 'em in Vietnam." The incompetence he witnessed in the Ninth Marines was one factor which led Johnson to question whether there was any clear American policy in Vietnam. Another was the dismissal of an officer whom Johnson considered to be an exceptional leader:

> One lieutenant taught his troops Marx and Mao. Said

"you'd better know the ideology you're fighting against."
Somebody wrote a letter home and said he was teaching
the boys communism and they [the Marine Corps] made
him resign his commission. Along about that time I
[started] to get slightly disillusioned. I thought, "These
people are crazy. Not only the people we're supposed to
be helping, but our own people are absolutely goddamn
stark raving bananas."[35]

Ernestine Thornton, who had been serving in Korea and
requested assignment to Vietnam, was unprepared for the
conditions under which she treated casualties near Saigon. She
remembered "mass confusion," with part of her hospital on
trucks and part of it in tents, and "a great deal of sameness;
hard, brutal work, twelve hours a day, seven days a week." Not
knowing the names and faces of the men she worked on, because
there were so many of them, greatly distressed her. During the
month of November 1966, five thousand casualties were run
through her system, the 85th Evacuation unit. "There really was
no escape from the war for nurses," Thornton remembered. At
times she worked all day and all night. On one occasion,
Thornton could not continue her duties in the Intensive Care
Unit because she was so fatigued she could no longer distinguish
between the positive and negative gauges on intravenous
machines or respirators. "Younger nurses," said Thornton, "were
already [in 1966] beginning to question, 'What are we doing here?
Why are we messing with these people?'" Thornton refused even
to consider that the "mighty U. S. Army wasn't doing the best
that they could for the people of South Vietnam." Later, in 1969–
70, she seriously began to question the war and the Army and
"was becoming bitter and cynical." Given the primitive
conditions under which she and other doctors and nurses
operated, Thornton wonders to this day "how we saved the
number of people that we did . . . . I saw things that would
exhaust the trauma team at Charleston General."[36]

Eventually Ernestine Thornton was transferred to Walter
Reed Hospital in Bethesda, Maryland as head nurse of an
amputee ward. She remained in that position for three years and
considered the assignment "probably the best work that I did in
the Army, 'cause these were the fellows I saw get well."
Thornton treated an increasing number of wounded veterans who
had been embittered by their experience in Vietnam, including
some who formed the nucleus of the Vietnam Veterans Against
the War [VVAW]. "I encountered more and more men who had
gone over and given parts of themselves and who asked 'why in

the hell are we doing this'?"[37]

The wounded veterans' question also verbalized the apprehensions under which the American people labored as United States military involvement escalated and began to appear endless. On the absurd stage of combat American soldiers encountered situations which destroyed for many of them their accepted notions about conduct under fire, and they responded accordingly. At home, the American people faced the betrayal of the nation's idealistic sense of mission as their government increasingly channeled national resources into an incomprehensible war. Chapter II investigates more closely the nature of the conflict in Vietnam and the responses of West Virginia combat soldiers. Further, it outlines the political formulation upon which American policy in Vietnam was constructed, and the conflict between Americans' self-perception and the realities of Vietnam. This conflict contributed to the nation's rejection of those soldiers who carried out the government's policies in Southeast Asia. It also fostered social and political alienation among a significant proportion of West Virginia Vietnam veterans, who struggled, knowingly or unknowingly, as both the victims and representatives of colonialism.

# Notes, Chapter I

[1]Lawrence M. Baskir and William A. Strauss, *Chance and Circumstance: The Draft, The War, and the Vietnam Generation* (New York: Alfred A. Knopf, 1978), p.3.

[2]Steven L. Giles, "Appalachia's Forgotten Warriors," quoted in Daniel L. Sumrok, Steven L. Giles, and Mildred Mitchell-Bateman, "Public Health Legacy of the Vietnam War: Post Traumatic Stress Disorder and Implications for West Virginians," *The West Virginia Medical Journal* 79 (September, 1983), p. 194.

[3]Charleston *Daily Mail*, May 26, 1980. Sumrok, Giles, and Mitchell-Bateman, "Public Health Legacy," p. 196.

[4]David M. Bonior, Steven M. Champlin, and Timothy S. Kolly, *The Vietnam Veteran: A History of Neglect* (New York: Praeger, 1984), p. 109.

[5]Baskir and Strauss, *Chance and Circumstance*, p. 4.

[6]John Gaventa, *Power and Powerlessness: Quiescence and Rebellion in an Appalachian Valley* (Urbana, Chicago, London: University of Illinois Press, 1980), pp. 34-35. Harry Caudill, *Night Comes to the Cumberlands: A Biography of a Depressed Area* (Boston and Toronto: Little, Brown and Company, 1963), p. 38. Sumrok, Giles, and Mitchell-Bateman, "Public Health Legacy," p. 201.

[7]C. Vann Woodward, *Origins of the New South, 1877-1913* vol. 9 of *A History of the South*. Baton Rouge: Louisiana State University Press, 1951), pp. 291-2. Caudill, *Night Comes to the Cumberlands*, pp. 60-62. John Alexander Williams, *West Virginia and the Captains of Industry* (Morgantown: West Virginia University Library, 1976) p. 1.

[8]John Alexander Williams, *West Virginia: A Bicentennial History* (New York: W. W. Norton & Company, Inc., 1976), pp. 199-203; Harry Caudill, "The Corporate Fiefdom: Poverty and the Dole in Appalachia," *Commonweal* 89 (January 24, 1969), p. 523; *Coal Government of Appalachia* (Charleston, West Virginia: Student Task Force for Appalachian Research and Defense Fund, 1971), p. 32. See also Tom Miller and Harry Baisden, "Who Owns West Virginia?" The Huntington *Herald-Dispatch*, December 22-29, 1974.

<sup>9</sup>Robert Blauner, "Internal Colonialism and Ghetto Revolt," *Social Problems* 16 (Spring, 1969): 397. Helen Lewis, "Fatalism or the Coal Industry: Contrasting Views of Appalachian Problems," *Mountain Life and Work* XLVI (December, 1970): 11. For a discussion of barrio colonialism, see Joan W. Moore, "Colonialism: The Case of the Mexican-Americans," *Social Problems 71 (Spring, 1970). pp. 463-72.*

<sup>10</sup>Baskir and Strauss, *Chance and Circumstance, pp. 8-9.*

<sup>11</sup>Ibid., p. 9.

<sup>12</sup>Ibid., pp. 9-10.

<sup>13</sup>Kai Erikson, *Everything in Its Path: Destruction of Community in the Buffalo Creek Flood* (New York: Simon and Schuster, 1976), p. 86.

<sup>14</sup>Interview with Randy Bowles, Huntington, West Virginia, September 22, 1984.

<sup>15</sup>Interview with Dave Evans, Charleston, West Virginia, November 10, 1984.

<sup>16</sup>Interview with Bill Fox, Huntington, West Virginia, November 17, 1984.

<sup>17</sup>Interview with James Hill, Charleston, West Virginia, September 27, 1984.

<sup>18</sup>Interview with Harry Beam, Huntington, West Virginia, February 11, 1985.

<sup>19</sup>Interview with Ernestine Thornton, Charleston, West Virginia, November 21, 1984.

<sup>20</sup>Interview with Roger Sanford, Huntington, West Virginia, September 11, 1984.

<sup>21</sup>Interview with Rick Richards, Charleston, West Virginia, November 10, 1984.

<sup>22</sup>Evans interview.

<sup>23</sup>Interview with Doug Johnson, Huntington, West Virginia,

May 15, 1986.

[24]Interview with John Williams, Huntington, West Virginia, October 13, 1984. See also, interview with Glen Hager, Huntington, West Virginia, September 17, 1984; Evans interview; Johnson interview.

[25]Fox interview.

[26]Ibid.

[27]Interview with Al Van Dyke, Charlottesville, Virginia, July 16, 1985.

[28]Sanford interview.

[29]Jack Weller, *Yesterday's People: Life in Contemporary Appalachia* (Lexington: University of Kentucky Press, 1965), p. 37. For a view of Appalachian fatalism, *see also* Richard Ball, "A Poverty Case: The Analgesic Subculture of the Southern Appalachians," *American Sociological Review* 33 (December, 1968), pp. 885–95; Ellen J. Stekert, "Focus for Conflict: Southern Medical Beliefs in Detroit" in Americo Paredes and Ellen Stekert, eds., *The Urban Experience and Folk Tradition* (Austin: University of Texas Press, 1971), p. 117. Stekert traced the survival of traditional Appalachian medical belief and practices into urban America, with conclusions similar to those of Sumrok, Giles, and Mitchell-Bateman.

[30]Beam interview.

[31]Gaventa, *Power and Powerlessness*, viii; Helen Lewis, "The Colonialism Model" in Helen Lewis, Linda Johnson, and Don Askins, eds., *Colonialism in Modern America: The Appalachian Case* (Boone, North Carolina: The Appalachian Consortium Press, 1978), pp. 12–14; Evans interview.

[32]Sumrok, Giles, and Mitchell-Bateman, "Public Health Legacy," pp. 193–94. Richards interview.

[33]Sanford interview.

[34]Bowles interview.

[35]Johnson interview.

[36]Thornton interview.

[37]Ibid.

# To Oppose Any Foe: American Credibility and the Seeds of Estrangement in Appalachian Vietnam Veterans

Being an American soldier, early in the Vietnam conflict, implied committing oneself to "whatever was required to insure that our fundamental freedoms would not be lost." Although the threat of monolithic communism had been lessened by the nationalist movements in emerging nations, two generations of Americans had ignored that reality and hardened their anti-communism into a series of conditioned reflexes which mandated fighting perceived communist aggression on any front.[1] However, for many Appalachian veterans, geopolitical factors became increasingly meaningless as they endured their tour of duty in Southeast Asia. The conflict between the ideological underpinnings of United States policy and their own sense of morality led to emotional and ethical struggles in those who could not reconcile America's mission in Vietnam with the realities of the war.

Largely as a result of the complex network of military, social, political, and ethical ambiguities which highlighted the Vietnam era, no ideological consensus regarding the war has emerged among Vietnam veterans. Confusion over the reasons for American military intervention in Vietnam combined with the growing opposition to the war on the home front to undermine the combat soldier's faith in his leadership, trapping him in the middle of a conflict between the nation's idealistic self-image and the conduct of the war. To the American people, "Vietnam" became synonymous with betrayal, inefficiency, stupidity, and loss of faith. The American combat soldier, whose role was to carry out policies and tactics devised more with an eye to geopolitical concerns than to clear military objectives, became a pawn for the tactics conceived by frustrated civilian and military planners who were unprepared for the abilities and will of the enemy's forces. American soldiers, increasingly alienated from a sense of mission, also became estranged from the American public who, by means of electronic media, saw the combat troops as the practitioners of those desperate tactical measures. One veteran, describing the Army as "a mirror image of a cross section of America," surmised that the "cross section" was disturbed at its own reflection and deflected its guilt to American soldiers. Practices alien to the concept of a just war such as body counts, search and destroy missions, and napalm bombings unsettled the American conscience. Whether as the visible symbols of a brutal conflict or as symbols of a political war which could not be won, Vietnam veterans became the recipients of the guilt and frustration of a public which failed to distinguish between the war and the warrior.[2]

Many veterans from West Virginia shared in the typical veteran's sense of betrayal at the suspension in Vietnam of a learned moral code and at the responses they encountered from the American people. One such veteran bitterly recalled that the military:

> . . . put me in a situation where I had to do things that were against my religious beliefs and morality. I didn't want to burn peoples' houses and villages. I've seen people on Cabin Creek who's just as hard up as those people [were.] I wouldn't burn their house. I didn't want to do it. That's what makes me angry. I was doing what my country told me to do. I was being a patriot; you're saying "Okay. It's okay to do it. You guys go ahead and do it." Then when [we] came home, they blame[d us] for every damn thing [we'd] done. It's not like the general got the blame in the rear. On TV you didn't see a general Zippoing a hooch. You saw a PFC Zippoing this damn hooch, right?[3]

To the GI it often appeared as if all of Vietnam was hostile, or at best indifferent. Politics, patriotism, and ethics became increasingly remote as country boys and ghetto kids struggled to wage war and survive in an alien culture. A Huntington veteran who was in Vietnam in 1966-67 believed that the Vietnamese people "could [not] care less when it comes to weighing communism against democracy, which is, of course, the main idea of why we were over there." The average Vietnamese, he observed, was worried primarily with feeding himself and his family. "He's not out there flag-waving, saying 'down with communism, up with democracy.' His motivation, whether he be a soldier or civilian, was simply to survive from the standpoint of whoever was in control." This veteran's observations were repeated by many others who perceived the war as a struggle for survival, by Americans and Vietnamese alike.[4]

Some veterans were troubled by the damage done to the Vietnamese culture by the American presence there. One commented on the destruction of the agricultural cycles in a village near DaNang, where he was based. The war had uprooted the residents of this village, called "Dogpatch" by American GIs, from their ancestral lands and their traditional dependence on the earth, the basis of what writer Frances Fitzgerald called the Vietnamese social contract. Through ancestral rites connected to land use, said Fitzgerald, Vietnamese children repeated the life cycles of their parents and grandparents, in turn transmitting them to their own children. "In this passage of time that had no history," wrote Fitzgerald, "the death of a man marked no final end." Buried in the rice fields that sustained his family, the father lived in the bodies of his descendants. The land, the one constant element to the Vietnamese, was sacred. The Vietnamese seldom left their village in peace time; to do so was to remove oneself from society. Fitzgerald argued that Americans "live in a society of replaceable parts, but the Vietnamese lived in a society of particular people, all of whom knew each other by their place in the landscape." Policies such as free-fire zones, relocation, the use of defoliants, and American efforts to root out and destroy the "Viet Cong infrastructure" (VCI) with search and destroy missions, disrupted and frequently destroyed the Vietnamese bond to the land, thereby creating resentment to the American presence in the countryside.[5]

Destroying the basis of Vietnamese life and culture may have been particularly devastating to some Appalachian veterans, whose cultural heritage included strong kinship and environmental bonds. Psychologist Kai Erikson has suggested that isolation contributed to the importance of family ties in appalachian communities. In a practical sense, he said, the family is a community unto itself, "one's only shelter in a hostile land." Appalachian families, according to Erikson, were not structured along lines of demonstrative personal intimacy but rather as a "generalized entity," from which each member "drew some measure of warmth and to which every member offered some measure of allegiance." The bond might appear almost impersonal, with family members knowing each other less as individuals than as part of the generalized family entity. When they were separated from family Appalachians felt greatly diminished as persons, "adrift, vacant, without a secure enough sense of their surroundings to know quite who they were." The traditional Appalachian family structure was one of extensive, complex neighborhoods which formed mutual aid societies. They were isolated, stable, and self-sustaining, stressing independence and cooperation. The kinship network served as a defensive mechanism against outside forces such as industrialization. Loyalties to family took precedence over civic responsibilities.[6] The Cabin Creek GI mentioned earlier experienced guilt burning down the hooches of isolated Vietnamese families in part because these unjustified acts of war challenged the moral standards he developed while growing up in similar circumstances. Doug Johnson of Huntington experienced similar cultural conflict upon witnessing the damage done to Vietnamese culture by the American military presence. He was struck by the spectacle of villagers fighting over food scraps in a garbage dump in "Dogpatch:"

> I'm talking about people who were not so much dispossessed or burnt out or in refugee camps, but [about] what our culture did to them. They stopped growin' rice. They stopped farmin'. They could go over and get more out of the garbage to eat that was still good . . . . I didn't really understand what was going on, I knew we were doing something to these people, I thought, "Why are they not farming?" And it was because they could make a bigger killing with less work on the garbage and slop we were throwing away. And we had annihilated what they'd been doing for thousands of years.[7]

Johnson also participated in operations in which entire Vietnamese villages were destroyed. Appalled at what he saw, he developed serious doubts about the justification for the American mission in Vietnam. "What wasn't burnt down or blown up," said Johnson, "[we] removed from the face of the earth . . . [we] moved every person out of there that wasn't killed." A way of life that had existed there "for God knows how many years" was in one instance destroyed in less than forty-five minutes. Ironically, Johnson and others gradually developed a stronger identification with the people whose culture they had disrupted than with the remote bureaucrats and strategists who had sent them to Vietnam.[8]

American soldiers were often put in the position of oppressing the people they were supposed to be helping. Sometimes the oppression was overt and brutal; sometimes it was more subtle. Glen Hager, a Navy veteran who volunteered for shore duty in Vietnam because he "wanted to get in the game," not "be on the sidelines," recalled a specific event which clarified for him the clash of America's supposed role in Vietnam and the reality of the American presence. Hager, who later became a counselor in the Huntington Veterans Outreach Center, remembered the vivid impression made upon him when he observed an incident between an American MP and an elderly Vietnamese woman. To Hager, it symbolized the futility of the American experience in Vietnam:

Once when I was on bus guard duty escorting the South Vietnamese workers that we had on our compound [out of the gates], Security searched everyone, searched all the Vietnamese, and took an apple from an old Vietnamese woman. Then it struck me. "What the hell *are* we doing [here], these are the people that we're supposed to be saving."[9]

Hager observed "patterns of abuse," implicit and explicit, by American soldiers under constant stress because of the nature of the war and their uncertainty as to the loyalties of the Vietnamese civilians. Struck by the irony of American soldiers at odds with "the people that we were willing to sacrifice our lives for," he consciously began to oppose the war. The erosion of the sense of duty and obligation with which American soldiers had been indoctrinated, and which Hager and others called into question, was summed up by Robert Muller of the Vietnam Veterans of America. "How the hell are you gonna' win the hearts and minds of these people when you conduct the most massive bombing campaign in history on top of their heads, and convert one-third of them into refugees, and kill a couple million of them?"[10]

American forces had been trained to fight an easily identifiable enemy in conventional warfare in which a piece of land was fought for and won or lost. In Vietnam, however, land might be taken and then given up. Units often pulled away from an area to fight somewhere else, then return to retake the same land forfeited earlier. Vietnam became "an endless war with rarely seen foes and no ground gains, just a constant flow of troops in and out of the country." The only measurable result "was an interminable production of maimed, crippled bodies and countless corpses." Such conditions fostered widespread rage and frustration in American troops, leading to mistrust and violence toward the Vietnamese, military authority, and toward "the society that sent [them] to Vietnam and then would not support them."[11]

Harry Beam was directly involved in one of the most visible and tragic episodes, the assault on Hamburger Hill, that illustrated the futility of the war and the frustration of its warriors. Beam's recollections of the situation summarized the suspicions of soldiers in the field when faced with the ambiguities of Vietnam:

There was so much flak back here [in the states] in terms of political controversy, primarily originated by enemies [in the press and antiwar movement], but a decision was made that once the hill was taken to move everyone on. They [North Vietnamese Army] moved back in . . . at the same time we had our first man walking on the moon, I was trying to get [permission to get] a gun to go back up that hill to take it back again. I was personally restricted in that process; I definitely had the impression that the units in my area were to some extent restricted.[12]

Hamburger Hill, said Beam, was "highly controversial, in that roughly 300 Americans died trying to take that hill the first time." The rationale for taking Hamburger Hill, he noted, was its location at the northern end of the Ashau Valley, literally dominating "all avenues of approach from [North] Vietnam." "Was it worth it?" asked Beam. "I don't know. I don't think one can truly evaluate just how many lives one is willing to spend for a piece of land." When the hill was finally taken, the Americans were ordered to abandon it.[13]

Given this and similar experiences, Beam was highly critical of American political leadership in Vietnam. "Any time you commit forces to war," he said, "there can be only one clear-cut objective; decisive military victory. If that's not the goal, then you don't need a military force, what you need is a bunch of highly paid policemen." Beam also commented on the issue of America's national will. For the first two or three years, the American people supported military action in Vietnam. "But they reach a point," said Beam, "and rightfully so, where they are asking themselves, 'why are our people going over there and dying? What are we achieving? The goal is not in sight.' You lose national will."[14]

Not only did combat soldiers in Vietnam fight under confusing political circumstances, but the guerilla nature of the war precluded knowing exactly who was the enemy. American troops were sometimes compelled to kill women and children, some of whom were actual combatants or Viet Cong operatives, but many of whom were innocent victims. The horror of the unknown enemy led to tragic consequences for many, including Doug Johnson. Due to his slight build, on several occasions Johnson was assigned duty as a "tunnel rat" and required to descend into passageways dug under Vietnamese settlements used by the Viet Cong for storing men and materiel. As Johnson discovered, the tunnels were also used by Vietnamese civilians for refuge. "When we'd go into a village and we'd find [tunnels]," said Johnson, "first thing we'd do is grab some woman by the back of the neck, twist up her hair and push her toward that hole . . . if she started backpedalin' you knew right away somebody was in there." In the village of An Lang, Johnson's patrol discovered "a whole mess of these tunnels" and Johnson was ordered to investigate the contents. "I was gettin' ready to drop down inside when I heard something and I went 'shit.'" Suspecting Viet Cong were in the tunnel, Johnson threw "three or four hand grenades . . . and I heard this cryin' and whimperin' and screamin' goin' on, I thought 'shit.' I could tell right away it was kids." When Johnson started down into the tunnel, a 120 mm rocket hit the hut, killing the two Marines with him and burying him in the tunnel with four dying Vietnamese children. "I think the oldest might have been four. The youngest was seven months old, maybe. There was an air hole, and I could get air through that. I had my flashlight." Johnson tore up his uniform.

> A coupla' these kids had lost arms and I tried to tie their arms back on. I did mouth-to-mouth [resuscitation] with two of 'em but all four of 'em died. And I was buried in that hole with 'em six or seven hours before anyone realized I was missin'. And I was almost crazy. I lost my mind down there, in that hole. I know I lost my soul, I know that. And after that, I changed. I got to be one real hard core son-of-a-bitch. They let me go on operations but I didn't talk to nobody.[15]

The fate of Vietnamese children weighed heavily on many veterans, perhaps because some have children whom they suspect are themselves victims of the war, either from the psychological scars inflicted upon their fathers or by physical and emotional difficulties which may be related to chemical contamination. One who feared the effects of the war on his children was David Smythers of Kenova, West Virginia, who was exposed to dioxin in the defoliant Agent Orange on several operations. Smythers was an artillery loader during an intensive siege at Khe Sanh, which lasted thirty-nine days, though "it may have been longer; it seemed like an eternity. We just continually shot those guns, *continuous*." To break the monotony of constantly loading artillery pieces, his commanding officer told Smythers to take a turn firing the weapon. "A guy over the radio said 'good shootin' David. You got six.' Well, I jumped up and down for joy," said Smythers. "It was like jumpin' up for your team scorin' at football. I might've killed little kids or anything. And [I] have to live with that every day."[16]

In addition to the horrors of the war itself many Vietnam veterans continued to be haunted for years by their experiences. John P. Wilson, a psychologist at Cleveland State University, has explained some of the reasons for veterans' difficult readjustment to civilian life. In 1978, Wilson published a five-volume treatise entitled *The Forgotten Warrior Project*, funded by the Disabled American Veterans. Wilson interviewed nearly a thousand Vietnam veterans in order to document their war experiences and the impact of those experiences on the veterans' postwar lives. Testifying before the United States Senate Committee on Veterans Affairs in 1980, Wilson profiled returned Vietnam veterans, in an effort to promote public awareness of a psychological difficulty, Post Traumatic Stress Disorder, endured by many of the Vietnam veterans.

Wilson presented to the Senate committee his explanation of a worst-case scenario, asking the senators to imagine being "demonic and powerful enough" to want to "make someone crazy." First, said Wilson, you would send a young man just out of high school to a confusing and unpopular war far away from home. Then, expose him to "intensely stressful events, some so horrible that it would be impossible to really talk about them later to anyone else except fellow 'survivors'." Further, you would create a one-year tour of duty during which the combatant flies to and from the war zone singly, without a cohesive, emotionally supportive unit with high morale. The one year tour, said Wilson, would also serve to instill a "survivor mentality" which would undermine an ideological commitment to winning the war and "seeing it as a noble cause." At DEROS, you would "rapidly remove the combatant and singly return him to his front porch without an opportunity to sort out the meaning of the experiences with the men in his unit"; there would be no public celebrations. Then, Wilson continued, you would make sure the veteran is stigmatized and portrayed to the public as a "drug-crazed psychopathic killer." Because of the inequities of the Selective Service System, the veteran would find it difficult to "reenter the mainstream of society because he is undereducated and lacks marketable job skills." Since the war was so traumatic to the nation, there would be no structure of support systems in society for the veteran, "especially among health professionals at Veterans Administration hospitals who would find his nightmares and residual war-related anxieties unintelligible." Finally, you would establish a GI Bill with inadequate benefits to pay for education and job training, all within a weak economy of high inflation and unemployment. Then, you would want the veteran to feel isolated, stigmatized, unappreciated, and exploited for being enough of a "sucker" to serve in an unpopular war. "Tragically," Wilson concluded, "this scenario is not fictitious; it was the homecoming for most Vietnam veterans."[17]

Another psychologist, Charles E. Figley, added to Wilson's analysis with the view that estrangement is a reciprocal process. Far from being the recipients of the heroic welcome home of American veterans from other wars, Vietnam veterans, as warriors from a stalemated war, were justified in concluding that "perhaps the best thing is to slink home quietly and unnoticed." Vietnam veterans became the scapegoats of a nation feeling guilt over the conduct of the war and rage over the progress of the war. Peace activists and hawks alike singled out returning vets for approbation. World War II veterans were wary of and often chastised them; others simply ignored them.[18]

As Wilson and Figley asserted, most Vietnam veterans, including those from the typically homogeneous communities of Appalachia, had little or no opportunity to "decompress" following their tour in Vietnam. The solitary return home was one of the unforeseen problems associated with the DEROS system. A Huntington veteran who returned home on Christmas Eve, 1970, recalled that "what they say about coming back alone, that's true in my case. I did come back alone, really just wanted to slip in."[19] Ironically, one West Virginia veteran who believed he did benefit from the opportunity to sort out his feelings and tensions about the war was able to do so only because of his debilitating wounds, necessitating a lengthy recovery period. "The time I spent in the hospital was good for me," he concluded. "Being with the other amputees for so long gave us a chance to deal with our problems and sort out our feelings on the war before going home." Upon leaving the hospital, however, he felt like he was "in the Twilight Zone. There I was, standing on the corner on my new legs, and people were walking by like there wasn't a war going on."[20] A Charleston area veteran, more typically, had no opportunity to work through his Vietnam experiences before being back home:

> One minute, be in the damn jungle. Sixteen hours later, walk in your parents' home, your wife's home, and "hello, how are you?" Sixteen hours before you were gunning some mother down and he was shooting at you. People showed no compassion, they didn't want to show understanding, I think the whole nation for a long time [was on] a guilt trip; the war was lost, there was no band playing, no red carpet. My biological father came home

from World War II, there was a damn band playing, and I don't think he done anymore in his war than I done in my war. In fact, he sat on his ass in the South Pacific.[21]

David Bonior, a United States Congressman from Michigan and a Vietnam era veteran, in 1984 published a study of the postwar experiences of Vietnam veterans entitled *The Vietnam Veteran: A History of Neglect*. During the 1970s, wrote Bonior, there prevailed in America a "deep national unease" which was revealed in national polls; for example, a 1972 Louis Harris poll found that 61% of Americans viewed Vietnam as an unwinnable war. Forty-nine percent agreed that Vietnam veterans were suckers, manipulated into risking their lives in "the wrong war, in the wrong place, at the wrong time."[22]

In the wake of the Vietnam experience, said Bonior, America's "national psyche" demanded a retreat from international involvement. Concurrently, Americans, unable to separate the Vietnam veteran from the Vietnam war, retreated from the returned veterans. According to Robert Muller of the Vietnam Veterans of America, the American people "ran a number on Vietnam veterans." The reluctance of the public to face the realities of Vietnam "made it socially unacceptable to mention the fact . . . that we were Vietnam veterans. Whenever we brought it up, you walked away from the conversation."[23]

The war in Indochina, markedly different from what Americans expected wars to be, weakened the psychological commitment necessary to sustain an extended war effort. The national attitude during Vietnam contradicted the spirit of solidarity which had prevailed in 1941, for example, after the Japanese attack on Pearl Harbor.[24] So bewildered were Americans by "what was happening to them and by what they themselves were doing," wrote one social critic, "that many came to believe that both in Indochina and at home the United States had been overtaken by a wholly accidental and, therefore, wholly absurd fate."[25]

Beliefs held sacred by Americans who had faith in the morality and basic goodness of their nation and its leadership were called into question by the trauma of Vietnam. When John F. Kennedy proclaimed in his 1961 inaugural address that America would "pay any price, bear any burden, oppose any foe" in order to insure the survival and success of liberty, the American people generally expressed little reservation in accepting the national role of guarantor of freedom throughout the world.[26]

Kennedy had a particularly strong impact on the people of

West Virginia, where his dramatic victory in the 1960 Democratic primary confirmed the broad base of his appeal. Running against the popular Hubert Humphrey, Kennedy captured the imagination of West Virginians during two campaign trips to the state, in which he demonstrated genuine concern for West Virginia's economic hardships. Kennedy, a Catholic, deliberately confronted the specter of religious bigotry which was expected to damage his chances in the Appalachian Bible belt. Emphasizing the spirit of freedom and pride in mountain people, Kennedy praised the patriotism and courage of West Virginians, commenting repeatedly on the sacrifices the state's young men had made in three wars. "If there is one quality which I think this state can be justly proud of," said the Senator, "it is the quality of courage. This is a state which has sent men to die in every section of the world . . . . In West Virginia you have a great opportunity to discuss the issues and the brightest days are ahead. This country was made by people who are willing to put it [sic] on the line."[27]

John Kennedy's charm and enthusiasm embodied the idealism of Americans and their faith in the virtue of their institutions and leaders. He cultivated a "sense of national euphoria, righteousness, [a] sense of goodness, mission. When these guys [our leadership] said something to us," said Robert Muller, "we said 'sure.' We had no reason by and large to doubt [their] honesty and integrity." Kennedy especially inspired young people with his vigorous patriotism. West Virginia congressman Ken Hechler wrote that Kennedy "awakened in young Americans an interest in and awareness of their government, the necessity to participate, and the nature and value of our nation's ideals . . . . He quickened the appreciation and understanding which young people hold for the Nation's [sic] noblest virtues." Shortly before Kennedy's historic primary triumph, one West Virginia columnist described him as "a storybook candidate. If teenagers could vote, only ['American Bandstand' disc jockey] Dick Clark could beat him."[28]

Following Kennedy's assassination in 1963, Americans' faith in their leadership was reinforced by President Lyndon Johnson's vision of the Great Society, the broad system of social reform conceived as a structure from which to build an America free of racial and class hostilities and to wipe out poverty. Johnson declared the War on Poverty in March 1964, affirming that "today for the first time in our history we have the power to strike away the barriers to full participation in our society." Appalachia was a testing ground for the Great Society. Kennedy's visits to West Virginia, and his appreciation for the critical primary victory, had convinced him that federal action was necessary to correct the legacy of poverty created by Appalachia's heritage of economic exploitation. Shortly before his death, he had appointed a panel to formulate a system for economic development in the region. That system was formally embodied as the Appalachian Regional Commission by President Johnson in 1965. The ARC has been criticized for fostering a professional bureaucratic elite disassociated from the poor, and attacked for evading "the whole question of economic colonialism, perhaps most serious since absentee ownership and control of Central Appalachia's one-industry coal economy is the taproot of the area's problems." Nonetheless, at its inception the ARC was a shining symbol of America's faith in inevitable progress and the goodness of its government. Young Appalachians looked to the future with hope, and were willing to defend their country when its leaders called.[29]

The Great Society, however, became another casualty of Vietnam. Johnson's political consensus for reform began to fragment and dissolve as the war expanded. Leaders of the civil rights movement broke with Johnson, and the War on Poverty was curtailed.[30] Civil rights activists were struck by the contradiction of America's seeming devotion to freedom in Vietnam at the cost of suspending its devotion to freedom in Mississippi. Advocates for the poor in Appalachia saw the energy generated by the War on Poverty channeled into the rice paddies and jungles of Southeast Asia. Lyndon Johnson's domestic vision had contributed to a reawakening of the ideal of active, enlightened government, "a faith in what men could do once they determined to control the conditions of their lives." Many Americans, wrote historian Thomas Powers, believed that the United States had arrived at "a qualitative turning point in history," that efforts to end poverty and racial injustice might "open the way to a new sort of national life."[31] The steadily rising costs of the war in Vietnam, however, undermined the promise of America to many of its people. Much of the hope for economic justice in the hollows of Appalachia evaporated as the sons of a depressed area marched off to Southeast Asia.

As the war continued to expand during 1966-68, declarations from the Johnson administration that the United States could afford guns *and* butter were refuted by policymakers in Washington. Conservatives in Congress insisted that Johnson cut back on the Great Society's agenda of domestic reform before they would grant him a requested ten-percent tax surcharge to finance the war. As Vietnam demanded more and more of the administration's attention and energy, Johnson became increasingly alienated from the civil rights movement and the ideals of the War on Poverty. The promise of America, said Senator Robert Kennedy, was dying for lack of spirit and money. The young idealists of the early 1960s, said Kennedy, were "now asked to kill in Southeast Asia where once they had been asked to regenerate the world."[32]

America's role in Vietnam and the constriction of the War on Poverty at home challenged the government's claim of commitment to economic and social justice. The ostensible aims of America's mission in Vietnam, i.e., the defense of freedom and the prevention of aggression by one nation upon another, lost their believability as the war widened. It soon became evident to most Americans that there was little or no political freedom in South Vietnam. As for fighting off external aggression, all of the combatants in the war besides Americans, with some allied South Korean and Australian support troops, were Vietnamese. The primary motivation for America in Vietnam became credibility: the need to demonstrate to the world an image of national strength and a consistent determination to use that strength on the international stage. Of all the war aims, that of protecting American credibility became the most important, particularly as the United States became entrenched in an increasingly difficult military situation.[33]

By the mid-1960s, as the War on Poverty was just beginning, the war had ceased to stand for anything other than the theory of credibility, which had been formulated by political and military strategists as a component of the doctrine of nuclear deterrence and containment of communism. The credibility theory affirmed that America must be prepared to demonstrate a willingness to use force against communist expansion, and to assure the communist powers that any nuclear attack would be met with swift and terrible retribution. Furthermore, any localized communist threat, if left unchallenged, would undermine the world's faith in America as the defender of freedom. In March 1965, Assistant Secretary of Defense John McNaughton summarized the doctrine, reporting that seventy-percent of America's reason for being in Vietnam was "to avoid a humiliating U. S. defeat" to the nation's reputation as guarantor of order in the world. Twenty-percent of the motivation for the war was to keep South Vietnam from falling under Chinese domination, and ten-percent was to "permit the people of South Vietnam to enjoy a better, freer way of life." McNaughton elaborated on this theme in January 1966. "The present U. S. objective in Vietnam is to avoid humiliation," he said. "The reasons why we went into Vietnam to the present depth are varied," he continued, "but they are now largely academic. Why we have *not* withdrawn is . . . one reason: To preserve our reputation as a guarantor [of anti-communism], and thus to preserve our effectiveness in the rest of the world."[34]

After Lyndon Johnson left office in 1968, President Richard Nixon reaffirmed the principle of credibility throughout his first term, vowing repeatedly to "preserve confidence in American leadership not only in Asia but throughout the world." John F. Kennedy's stirring invocation to fight any foe, so inspiring in the context of a nation confident of its magnanimity, cast an ominous shadow when viewed from the perspective of credibility. When optimistic predictions of speedy victory over the communist movement in Vietnam had given way to military reverses and drastic measures in the field, the strategists of credibility realized that the particulars of Vietnamese politics were more critical than they had anticipated. The architects of credibility, academic theorists and managers like W. W. Rostow, Robert McNamara, MacGeorge Bundy, and Henry Kissinger, had assumed that escalating the violence in the Vietnamese countryside would push the enemy to the breaking point. Actually, escalation strengthened the will of the Vietnamese revolutionaries while weakening the will of the American people and soldiers to inflict punishment.[35] Tragically, young Americans fought in the meatgrinder of Vietnam not for freedom at home or for Vietnamese liberation. They killed and died for global power abstractions conceived in closeted discussions among ambitious American chauvinists.

Those whose task it was to implement the doctrine of credibility on the ground were American soldiers, predominantly poor American soldiers from the ghettos, barrios, rural midwest, and hills and mining towns of Appalachia. As pawns in a geopolitical scheme, they were confronted by determined opponents driven by the goal of ridding their country of the vestige of colonialism. When the United States succeeded the French as the foreign power in Vietnam, America became the enemy of Vietnamese nationalism. Ironically, West Virginia soldiers, most of whom were subjects of an internal colonial system at home, were destined to become the military agents of external colonialism in Southeast Asia. The Vietnam war caused them, and the American people, in great degree to lose their "pervasive confidence that American arms and American aims were connected to justice and morality."[36]

When the decisions were made on Vietnam, the United States chose anti-communism, anti-nationalism, and pro-colonialism. When the difficulty of defeating the forces of Ho Chi Minh was finally impressed on the American military and civilian leaders, self-doubt and self-criticism by the American public grew. Traditional attitudes held by American soldiers relative to war and authority clashed with the realities the soldiers faced. The general pre-1968 Tet Offensive belief in the propriety of American interests and objectives was challenged by civilians and warriors alike. In Vietnam, wrote social historian Walter Capps, the American consensus came apart. The societal sense of shared purpose was decimated, the basis of American political motivation became unclear, and accepted concepts of society's general order were severely undermined. "The myth of America was broken," wrote Capps. "No one had any longer a firm hold on the American Dream."[37] The veterans of the Vietnam war became symbols of the shame of the nation. They were reminders of America's collective uncertainty. Their experience in the war enabled the veterans to "look deeply into the American soul where they witnessed the conflict, encountered the ambivalence, and were pulled by discordant motivations. The veterans were direct participants in the ritual act that signified the loss of American innocence."[38]

When the North Vietnamese Army and the Viet Cong launched the Tet Offensive in January 1968, a campaign on a scale of which the Johnson administration had insisted the enemy was incapable, American pretensions about its role in Vietnam were finally shattered. Although the American press failed to drive home the point of the serious losses the communist forces suffered during Tet, said Robert Muller, the importance of Tet was to demonstrate to the American people that their leadership had misrepresented the course of the war. "So the credibility of the administration was shot," said Muller. "That's when people said 'wait a minute, this is bullshit.'" Mainstream public opinion turned decidedly against the war, and Lyndon Johnson was compelled to leave office rather than face defeat in the 1968 election. Appalachian soldiers, who had believed in the fundamental goodness of their government, their military, and their people, witnessed the destruction of the American spirit in the jungles of Vietnam. They returned home to face the emotional, physical, and economic consequences of that erosion in their own communities. Said one West Virginia veteran, with the trauma of Vietnam "the consciousness of the whole United States was turned on its ear."[39]

To many Vietnam veterans, disillusioned at their experiences in the war and with the confusion of American policy there, the apparent betrayal of the American people by the nation's political leadership generated strong resentment and mistrust of authority.

Confidence in American institutions suffered. "There's so much hypocrisy [in government]," said a Huntington veteran. "And that's one thing that Vietnam veterans are keenly aware of. I started learning lessons real quick in Vietnam and in the service. I can spot phoniness, and it's all around . . . and the system really sucks. I developed that opinion while I was in Vietnam."[40] Bill Fox expressed similar opinions. Fox saw himself as a "warrior in an unjust war . . . it was stupid for us to be there. We just slaughtered each other for nothing. It's totally futile." Fox has a son born in 1980. Should he ever be faced with the decision whether or not to participate in a war, Fox would urge him to make a

> . . . thought-over decision, and not be like I was, which was a blind cow to the slaughter. I'm basically a pacifist now, because of the experience. I have a problem with trust in general. Politicians, they're a bunch of idiots, there's no difference in my mind between a Republican and a Democrat, they're all politicians. Self-serving, serving big business and other interests . . . our political system sucks. Maybe the system doesn't, but the way our system is run.

The country is run, said Fox, not by an enlightened government, but by multinational corporations which government serves. "Government serves commerce," he continued, "and anybody who doesn't see that is just awfully uninformed or naive."[41]

As a result of the disillusionment brought on by the Vietnam experience, the idealism of much of the "Vietnam generation," veteran and non-veteran, was supplanted by an often angry cynicism. That cynicism led inexorably to a high degree of alienation that was, according to David Addlestone, legal advisor to the Vietnam Veterans of America, "part of the Vietnam veteran's baggage." The next chapter will develop the theme of cultural alienation and investigate some of its implications for local Vietnam veterans when they returned to their communities. Hailing from small, relatively homogeneous communities, Appalachian veterans were anxious to put the war behind them and get on with their lives. Many discovered, however, that their combat experiences did not leave them. The clash between what they had known and believed before and came to know and believe in Vietnam often put them at odds with their non-veteran peers and their parents' generation who could not understand these soldiers who had "lost the war."[42]

# Notes, Chapter II

[1]Walter Capps, *The Unfinished War: Vietnam and the American Conscience* (Boston: Beacon Press, 1982), pp. 51-68.

[2]Interview with Harry Beam, Huntington, West Virginia, February 11, 1985.

[3]Interview with David Evans, Charleston, West Virginia, November 10, 1984.

[4]Interview with Maurice Clark, Huntington, West Virginia, September 20, 1984; also, Evans interview; interview with Glen Hager, Huntington, West Virginia, September 14, 1984; interview with Doug Johnson, Huntington, West Virginia, May 15, 1986.

[5]Frances Fitzgerald, *Fire in the Lake: The Vietnamese and the Americans in Vietnam* (New York: Random House, 1972), p. 11.

[6]Kai Erikson, *Everything In Its Path: Destruction of Community in the Buffalo Creek Flood* (New York: Simon and Schuster, 1976), p. 12. Helen Matthews Lewis, Sue Easterling Kobak, and Linda Johnson, "Family, Religion, and Colonialism in Central Appalachia, or Bury My Rifle at Big Stone Gap" in Helen Matthews Lewis, Linda Johnson, and Don Askins, eds., *Colonialism in Modern America: The Appalachian Case* (Boone, North Carolina: The Appalachian Consortium Press, 1978), pp. 115, 131.

[7]Johnson interview.

[8]Ibid.

[9]Hager interview.

[10]Public address by Robert Muller, Marshall University, Huntington, West Virginia, April 21, 1986.

[11]Jim Goodwin, *Continuing Readjustment Problems Among Vietnam Veterans: The Etiology of Combat Related Post Traumatic Stress Disorder* (Cincinnati, Ohio: Disabled American Veterans Press, 1984), p. 9.

[12]Beam interview.

<sup></sup>[13]Ibid.

[14]Ibid.

[15]Johnson interview.

[16]Interview with David Smythers, Kenova, West Virginia, April 3, 1985.

[17]John P. Wilson, cited in Myra MacPherson, *Long Time Passing: Vietnam and the Haunted Generation* (New York: Doubleday & Company, 1984), p. 227;

[18]Charles R. Figley and Seymour Leventman, *Strangers At Home: Vietnam Veterans Since The War* (New York: Praeger, 1980), p. xxix.

[19]Hager interview.

[20]Charleston *Gazette-Mail*, November 11, 1984.

[21]Interview with Jim Hill, Charleston, West Virginia, September 27, 1984.

[22]David M. Bonior, Steven M. Champlin, Timothy S. Kolly, *The Vietnam Veteran: A History of Neglect* (New York: Praeger, 1984), p. 35.

[23]Ibid., p. 35. Charleston *Gazette*, December 12, 1979.

[24]Paul Camacho, "From Hero to War Criminal: The Negative Image of the Vietnam Veteran," in Figley and Leventman, *Strangers At Home*, p. 268.

[25]Jonathan Schell, *The Time of Illusion* (New York: Praeger, 1980), p. 7.

[26]Ibid., p. 9.

[27]Charleston *Gazette*, May 5, 1960. Fairmont *Times*, April 19, 1960.

[28]Interview with Robert Muller, Washington, D. C., August 8, 1985. Hechler's tribute was reprinted from remarks he entered into the Congressional Record shortly after Kennedy's

assassination, under the title *West Virginia Memories of President Kennedy*, 1963, p. 41. The comment about Dick Clark was attributed to an anonymous reporter by columnist Don Marsh in a profile of Kennedy in the Charleston *Gazette*, May 7, 1960. For an in depth appraisal of the Kennedy campaign in West Virginia, *see* James McCrae Crews, Jr., *JFK and the Mountaineers: John F. Kennedy's Rhetoric in the 1960 West Virginia Presidential Primary* (Ph. D. dissertation, Florida State University, 1980.)

[29]John Gaventa, *Power and Powerlessness: Quiescence and Rebellion in an Appalachian Valley* (Urbana, Chicago, and London: University of Illinois Press, 1980), p. 162. Comment on the ARC from the Louisville *Courier-Journal*, April 11, 1973, cited in Gaventa, *Power and Powerlessness*, p. 163.

[30]Thomas Powers, *Vietnam: The War At Home* (Boston: G. K. Hall & Co., 1984), pp. 154-55.

[31]Ibid., p. 221.

[32]Ibid., p. 223.

[33]Schell, *The Time of Illusion*, p. 8.

[34]Ibid., p. 11.

[35]Ibid., pp. 63, 342-45, 360-61, 363, 367-69.

[36]Morris Dickstein, *Gates of Eden: American Culture in the Sixties* (New York: Basic Books, Inc., 1977), p. 271.

[37]Ibid. Capps, *The Unfinished War*, p. 14.

[38]Ibid., pp. 51-68.

[39]Muller interview. Evans interview.

[40]Hager interview.

[41]Interview with Bill Fox Huntington, West Virginia, November 17, 1984.

[42]Muller interview. Interview with David Addlestone, Washington, D. C., August 8, 1985.

# How Many Kids Did You Kill Today?
## Appalachian Vietnam Veterans
## at Home and on the Campus

The circumstances under which the United States escalated the war in Vietnam failed to capture the imagination of the American people or generate a unified response. Unlike previous wars, American involvement did not begin with a major event such as Pearl Harbor, which galvanized American public opinion in support of the war effort. Lyndon Johnson relied on the rhetoric of credibility and the tenuous justification of the Gulf of Tonkin incident to spur Congress and the public to acceptance of escalation. Consequently, as the war dragged on and a sense of purpose and victory became increasingly remote, public support for the war and its warriors began to collapse. After the Tet Offensive in 1968 Vietnam became an irrevocably "bad war" and the American people began to look for someone to bear the responsibility. The responses of the government and military establishment to the Vietnam debacle contributed to the estrangement of Vietnam veterans. Many returning soldiers struggled to reconcile the conflict between their personal ethics and the events of the war. Their emotional confrontation was intensified by a more subtle conflict pressed upon them by their own guilty nation. Like most Vietnam veterans, those from Appalachia encountered, with varying degrees of success, struggles in their attempts to reintegrate themselves into the American mainstream.[1]

The homecoming for Vietnam veterans was colored by the nation's effort to find scapegoats for the trauma of the war. Peace activists had directed most of their opposition to the war at the Johnson administration, but often failed to distinguish between opposition to Johnson's policy and those who were ordered to carry it out. After Tet, as Congressional support for the administration wavered, the executive began a campaign to shift the blame to the military establishment.[2] The military establishment, to deflect public approbation from itself, participated in the transmission of public war guilt to the veterans of the Vietnam war. A round of official "buck-passing" occurred, wrote psychologist Paul Camacho, "[and] flow[ed] naturally to the lower command levels. And [at] rock bottom was, of course, the enlisted man, the grunt, now labeled veteran." One West Virginia veteran revealed clearly that veterans understood what was being done to them. "The government wanted to blame us for losing the war," he recalled. "As long as we were whacked-out baby-killers, they could say 'well, listen, if we had better troops, we'd 'a done a better job.' Well, that's bullshit. If we had a better reason and a better cause, we'd 'a done a better job."[3]

In addition to absorbing from superior officers the blame for the war, Vietnam veterans also endured the injustices of the military discharge system. Among legal authorities, there is nearly complete agreement that the system of discharges was seriously abused by the military during the Vietnam war. A less than honorable discharge, called "bad paper" by veterans, is a stigma which follows a veteran throughout his/her life when seeking employment, and veterans with less than a General Discharge are barred from GI bill benefits. Over one-half million veterans received General or Undesirable Discharges during the Vietnam era. Undesirable and General Discharges are administrative decisions, sometimes dispensed without even a hearing. The necessity for the military to have a system of sanctions for misconduct is undeniable, but the potential for abuse in the military justice system is enormous. Never was this abuse more evident than in the case of Vietnam.[4]

Administrative discharges were used in Vietnam as a tool by which the military could avoid the difficulties of dealing with soldiers who displayed "problematic behavior." Vietnam, where the average age of the American combat soldier was 19.2 years, was the country's first teenage war. According to John Wilson of the *Forgotten Warrior Project*, this is a period in which most adolescents live through a "psychosocial moratorium," during which the individual establishes a "more enduring personality structure and sense of self." Young soldiers cut off from their home and culture, steeped in the idealism of an American moral crusade, were suddenly confronted in Vietnam with death and mutilation all around them. For the combat adolescent in Vietnam, the ambiguous and conflicting values associated with the nature of the war and his roles in it disrupted the period of personal development and often led to the problematic behavior the military wished to avoid. The administrative discharge was often a convenient means by which the military eliminated many individuals who were experiencing, among other problems, nascent psychological difficulties. The nature of the discharge, furthermore, could ensure that the government would not be liable for GI benefits when these difficulties became manifest. "The Marines are hard on people," said one West Virginia veteran. "I mean, if you get bad paper from the Marine Corps they'll [the VA, employers, peers, etc.] slam your ass big time."[5]

The American public, unable or unwilling to draw

distinctions between veterans with various types of discharges, for a time uniformly labeled them losers, baby-killers, and drug users who had lost the "little war." The stigma extended to Honorably Discharged veterans as well. Although the combat desertion rate among Vietnam veterans was lower than that of the veterans of any other war and approximately 70% of Vietnam veterans had been volunteers, both the patriotism and the courage of the Vietnam returnees came under fire from the public and, rather astonishingly, from the established veterans organizations. Vietnam veterans were especially unwelcome on college campuses in the late 1960's and early 1970s.[6]

Appalachian veterans endured the same difficulties upon returning home as did Vietnam veterans from other areas. Readjustment problems were not immediately recognized or accepted, however, either by the public or by private and government health agencies. "West Virginia," according to a staff psychologist at the Veterans Administration Hospital in Huntington, "is a state that is traditionally very patriotic. Veterans came home with a sense of having done their duty and went back to being farmers and coal miners, or whatever." West Virginia Vietnam veterans, he continued, easily made the transition from combat back to hometown because of the "close-knit nature" of the small communities in a rural state. "I just haven't seen the bitterness or the anger [among veterans] that is so popular today in movies and books." This bitterness might exist in "other cultural regions of the nation, like the metropolitan Northeast, but not in West Virginia."[7]

One might conclude from these observations, made in 1979, that Appalachian Vietnam veterans came home and went to work or school as if they had not been doing anything extraordinary for the past year. The comments of the staff psychologist might also reflect an institutional inability and/or unwillingness to recognize and treat the symptoms of Post Traumatic Stress Disorder, and a consequent attempt to diminish its validity. While it is true that most Vietnam veterans apparently have made a successful re-entry into civilian life, this should not obscure the reality that the obstacles to readjustment were initially understated, frequently ignored, and have only within the past few years been acknowledged institutionally or by the American public. The homecoming reality for many West Virginia veterans was summarized by a Kanawha Valley resident who returned home in 1971. That reality revealed a different perspective from that of the aforementioned VA psychologist:

The only one to meet me at Kanawha Airport when I

came home was my father. When I got home, I went for a walk down the hollow where I live. I wanted to talk about it, but nobody wanted to listen. I'm proud to be a Vietnam veteran. But there was a long time when I wasn't, when others wouldn't let me. It's a shame that after all these years I'm only now beginning to get help.[8]

Dr. Stephen Giles, who was team leader at the Huntington Veterans Outreach Center when the facility opened in 1980, observed that while the veterans of all wars have readjustment difficulties, the level and extent of the disapproval met by Vietnam veterans made their situation unique to the generations of American veterans. When Giles returned to college after serving in Vietnam, he "tried to disassociate [himself] from the war experience. Antiwar sentiment was perhaps stronger there than in many environments."[9]

Many Vietnam veterans underwent experiences similar to Giles when they returned to their respective colleges. According to Paul Camacho, "the [Vietnam] veteran [was] apprehensive upon entering college," maintaining a low profile. If possible, said Camacho, the veteran on campus "will remain low-keyed . . . [and] can thereby manage the 'tension information'; by not revealing himself as a member of a 'discreditable' status group, he avoids being considered a 'discredited' person. In short, he endeavors to pass."[10]

The experiences of West Virginia veterans confirmed the observations of Giles and Camacho. When Rick Richards of Charleston went to college upon his discharge from the Army in 1969, he carefully avoided mentioning that he was a Vietnam veteran. "It didn't help you socially," he said, "didn't help you get dates. And there's no way you can explain what it was like to someone who wasn't there."[11] Bill Fox experienced indignities at the hands of the military after his tour in Vietnam. Upon arrival at Edwards Air Force Base in California after a non-stop flight from Long Binh in Vietnam, Fox's first impression was of the insensitivity of the Army:

> The Army were real assholes . . . the first thing when we got back to Edwards they ran us through customs looking for dope. And that pissed everybody off. We'd just been in a war for a year and got shot at and now they don't trust us . . . . Ironically, of the two hundred of us on the airplane, they didn't even find one joint. And that kind of set the tone for my out-processing, you know.[12]

The insensitivity did not abate when Fox returned to civilian life. By the time he returned to Marshall University, Fox was strongly opposed to the war. He was reluctant, however, to speak of his status as a Vietnam veteran except to close friends, a reluctance he has overcome only within the last few years. "I didn't talk about 'Nam on purpose," Fox recounted, "because I wanted to fit in . . . my peers were against the war. And I wasn't against the war because they were against it. I was against it because of my experience there." His peers, particularly those active in antiwar activity, looked down on Vietnam veterans, especially those who had volunteered for the service, as he had. Ironically, Fox, who could speak for the peace movement out of direct experience, felt compelled to conceal much of his identity.[13]

Jeff Payne of Hurricane, West Virginia, enrolled at West Virginia University in the fall of 1968 after a tour in Vietnam. His previous tenure at WVU, in the early '60s, was marked by an absence of student protest or awareness about the war. He returned to a different atmosphere, reflective of increased public consciousness and passions in the wake of the Tet Offensive. He recalled:

> I went back in '68. I saw a great difference. The antiwar movement was really picking up. I didn't want to be on either side, I just wanted to move through . . . I didn't want to take a position. I didn't like what I had done, [but] I didn't think it was right or wrong at that point. I didn't want to be around those guys who wanted to talk about it all the time and I didn't want to be around the people who were against it.[14]

Payne and other Vietnam veterans were caught in ideological conflicts not only between other students but with professors as well. Payne specifically recalled getting into "a real screaming match" with an antiwar professor when the professor claimed that America would never defeat the forces of Vietnamese nationalism. Frustrated, Payne found himself in the position of defending the American mission in Vietnam even though "I knew that what I was saying was crap, this guy was right . . . he knew what he was talking about and I was coming from 7 1/2 months' experience in a little rice country." Payne experienced dissonance over America's stated objectives in Vietnam and the combat procedures in which he had been compelled to participate. He was convinced that the American presence in Vietnam brought no positive changes to the country and people, and he doubted that the destruction brought about by the war could ever be rectified.[15]

Glen Hager began taking classes at Marshall University after he was discharged from the Navy late in 1970. The employment picture was bad in Huntington, Hager said, and he decided to study counseling courses "until they [would] flunk me out." Hager "lucked into" some professors in counseling who encouraged him and influenced him to continue in the program, where he eventually earned a master's degree. Before entering the service, Hager had been interested in pursuing a career as an athletic coach. However, he said, "I just could not get back into the 'game plan'. It just seemed frivolous because I'd seen much more than I felt like I should've seen at that age."

Hager's counseling courses helped him work out some of the readjustment problems other Vietnam veterans were struggling with but did not get to talk about. The nature of counseling, said Hager, helped him communicate some of his sentiments about the war and his role in it. Still, he preferred to identify himself only as a veteran, not a Vietnam veteran, to his peers:

> Marshall had just gotten into the fad of the peace marches. It was real crazy for a Vietnam veteran to be there, and you didn't admit that you were one, necessarily. You had your groups of people marching through the classrooms, you know, just open up the door, you got ten or fifteen students marching through the aisles [chanting] . . . . That [situation] hurt the professors, but they had a way of . . . connin' themselves, actin' like everything was real cool. Now that the times are conservative they're on that bandwagon, too.[16]

Hager was opposed to the war but "had his own reasons" for his opposition. He and other Vietnam veterans, who could have been valuable allies to the antiwar movement, felt ostracized by what Hager called the "hippie element." Their ideas and his were quite close, he recalled, but he was angered by their rejection of veterans, their vilification of the human symbols of the war.[17]

The experiences of Ernestine Thornton further illustrated the abuses endured by Vietnam veterans from various elements of the American political spectrum. Thornton eventually consolidated strong suspicions of the military and the government, but in 1969-79 she was continuing her career as an Army nurse, assigned to Cincinnati as a recruiter. There she routinely encountered hostile antiwar demonstrators "everywhere I turned." She once had to await a Marine escort from her car to her office as the car was pelted with rotten eggs and vegetables. She was advised by her superiors not to wear her Army uniform or drive a government vehicle on recruiting trips. Later, as a nurse in rehabilitation at Walter Reed Hospital in Washington, she remembered some right-wing Washington tabloids which "specialized in giving rotten Vietnam stories, about GIs fragging officers, running, and hiding out on patrol." These attacks by the "yellow press," said Thornton, signified the low point of her Army career. As head nurse on an amputee ward, "I had fifty guys layin' out there without arms and legs who somehow or other had seen some combat."[18]

Lewisburg veteran John Williams volunteered for an additional six-months' duty in Vietnam in order to qualify for early release from his enlistment obligation. Had he returned to the United States at the conclusion of his original tour in Vietnam, Williams would have still had a year to serve stateside. He explained the decision to extend his tour. "I was so sick of the service. If I came back here [with time remaining on my enlistment], I'd probably get in trouble because I didn't see any way I could fit back into a strict military life and be tolerant of it." Williams perceived a "depressing" militarization of civilian life when he returned to West Virginia, noticing, for example, an alarming increase in the visibility of uniformed police in Huntington and Lewisburg. "It seemed like things were starting in the same direction here as what I'd experienced there. It . . . concerned me and turned me very much against the system at that time."[19]

When Williams landed at Edwards Air Force Base, "all they did really was check us for venereal disease, see if there was any drugs in our blood . . . and put us on the street." There was no deprogramming, Williams said, no plan to provide the veterans with the tools to re-enter civilian life. "And I was going to Lewisburg by about two in the afternoon. Thirty-six hours before that I'd been on duty in Vietnam." Williams underwent intense cultural alienation upon his return, unable to absorb adequately the values of his community after his experience in the service:

It was really strange because I just didn't fit in anywhere. I felt very withdrawn from everything. I couldn't comprehend the people around me anymore because life had taken on a whole different meaning for me after my experience. It seemed to me like everyone here is just living in a fantasy world. There's so many people here that just have no idea what's going on in the rest of the world.[20]

Williams went to Marshall University when he got out of the service but left after two semesters because "I felt very rejected by most of my peers . . . when they found out I was a Vietnam veteran. In some instances there was verbal abuse; much of the time it was just being ignored, like you weren't really a person." He "totally rejected" the college environment, leaving school [he has since returned to complete his degree program in English] because:

> A person can only be subjected to so much. You just don't want to stay. When I was young, we pledged allegiance to the flag every morning, said the Lord's Prayer, and believed in basic things . . . [such as] personal freedom. And, of course, the military's the exact opposite of that. The military's a dictatorship. You come out wanting an opportunity to formulate your own life. And you run into some of those basic attitudes that you experienced or were exposed to in the service . . . . You see the system as not at all what it was supposed to be or what you had been programmed to believe it would be. And it's very disillusioning. So I just dropped out.[21]

Many Vietnam veterans began experiencing the disillusionment with pre-service beliefs noted by John Williams long before they left the military, and carried this disillusionment into their civilian lives. Army Chaplain William Mahedy summarized the process of alienation, attributing it to a sense of guilt, the feeling of "having been victimized or scapegoated by the government, resistance to moral and spiritual authorities, cynicism toward institutions and authorities formerly believed and trusted." Mahedy concluded that these characteristics combined to dry up the veterans' "reservoir of moral resources. There is even alienation from one's feelings."[22]

The conflict experienced by soldiers in Vietnam over their mission was heightened by the erosion of traditional lines of authority within the service. Military discipline depends largely on the establishment within the ranks of positive, responsive, responsible, and authoritative leadership. During Vietnam, the services had difficulty in establishing and maintaining a sense of positive leadership. The corps of officers responsible on a daily basis for enlisted personnel and draftees was "badly strained" as the war escalated. General William Westmoreland commented as Army Chief of Staff that the demands of the war had "truly stretched the Army almost to its elastic limit. We had to lower our standards to meet the requirements in numbers." Responsibility for the morale and disciplinary crises, as well as the soldiers' welfare, fell, therefore, to young and inexperienced leaders. Enlisted men showing any promise of leadership ability were rushed through noncommissioned officers school and soon put in field command of eight-to-ten-man squads. Called "shake and bake sergeants," often just out of high school, they generally lacked the military knowledge and experience necessary to their roles.[23]

Inexperience together with the DEROS rotation policy undermined the establishment of solidarity within combat units. A fresh company commander had problems asserting his authority with troops who had already been in combat situations. By the time he overcame his inexperience, his DEROS was near. "His interest then lay in suppressing the outward manifestations of resistance and resentment, just getting by until the problems could be left to his replacement." Being of the same generation as the men they commanded, new officers were often reluctant to confront the antimilitary attitudes many of their troops developed or refined, particularly during escalation as the percentage of draftees in combat rose. The officers went along with anti-military modes of dress and behavior in their companies, further eroding the sense of discipline so critical to the military's positive leadership. During a year of legal defense work in Vietnam, attorney David Addlestone "encountered dozens of combat refusals and hundreds of minor acts of insubordination, almost always ending in little or no punishment."[24]

Those who fought in Vietnam were accustomed to the relaxation of the "spit and polish" of the regular military. Many continued to display a "distinctly unmilitary style: floppy hat, a slouching and slow moving walk," facial hair and non-regulation haircuts. Veterans with time left to serve on their military obligation could cause disciplinary problems. The "early out" option exercised by John Williams was as much an attempt by the services to keep Vietnam returnees away from new recruits as it was to retain experienced soldiers in Vietnam.[25]

Mark Moore of Huntington was stationed on the U.S.S. *Sierra* in Norfolk, Virginia in 1972-73, as the American troop count in Vietnam was being de-escalated under Richard Nixon's Vietnamization policy. Moore was intrigued by the distinctly non-military appearance and bearing of the Vietnam returnees he saw aboard the *Sierra*:

We had what was called a "transient personnel office." Guys who'd been in 'Nam would come on the *Sierra* and would have to wait out their time. And there were some real crazy people in that group, they were just different. They didn't have any respect for anything. They were just like, "I want out of here, I don't need this shit." They didn't have a real high profile, most of them kind of stuck to themselves.

They didn't say much about it. You could look at them and tell they were from [the war.] They had . . . tatoos on their arms and real faded shirts, and old baseball hats, and real faded jeans. They'd carry a big knife or something on their web-belts. There wasn't anybody that could do that much to them or say anything to them . . . they'd say "screw you. I don't need you."[26]

Those who came back from Vietnam with time left on their enlistment functioned within a military limbo. There was no real point in retraining them or giving them positions of responsibility. Many, however, were subjected to the daily routines of inspections, formations, and "petty harrassment" they had gone through as recruits, administered by commanding officers who likely had not been to Vietnam.[27] "They [officers] didn't want the veterans talking to the regular troops," said Rick Richards. "They had severe discipline problems with some of the returning Vietnam veterans." When commanders ordered Vietnam returnees to perform the "shit details" of the regular army, said Richards, the officers often met resistance. "The attitude [to] 'do this, do that'," he said, was often ". . . what the fuck you gonna' do? Send me to a combat zone?" Dave Evans concurred with Richards. When a soldier returned from Vietnam, said Evans, he faced resentment from officers who had not been to the war. This resentment might be particularly acute, said Evans, for the troop returning to his original platoon in the United States, under the command of his original officer. "He could see you were a different person. You were a survivor, and you couldn't be fucked with because if you didn't get killed in Vietnam, there's nothing they could do to hurt you here."[28]

Survivors of Vietnam often caused discomfort not only for their military superiors but for those around them in civilian life, a discomfort facilitated by the popular images of the "crazed killer." Members of his own family, Bill Fox remembered, "sort of looked at me funny, like they were waiting for me to flip out." Doug Johnson recalled being ostracized by the deacons of his childhood church, who informed him directly that he was not welcome at services. "They said I would be detrimental to the youth of the church. They said I would corrupt the kids, and they did not want me there because I would kill people." Johnson had not yet turned twenty-one, and "needed to feel like I fit someplace, and I couldn't even fit there."[29]

The American public was not prepared to recognize that the experiences of Vietnam veterans were different from the soldiers of other wars. Mental health analysts concluded that "a major problem has been to convince the public, both lay and professional, that Vietnam veterans . . . experienced a war that was unique in its situations and stresses."[30] The manifestations of that stress, though, were not immediately evident. Psychologist Peter Bourne found that through 1970 reports of psychiatric problems among combat personnel in Vietnam were significantly lower than those of World War II personnel. He concluded these figures could be attributed to several factors, including better medical care in the field, rapid medical treatment, "sporadic rather than continuous combat," and the one-year tour. Another factor, said Bourne, was that the military had attempted to redefine reality for the combat soldier, constructing an ideology designed to minimize stress. Soldiers were given a "more functional perspective," to help them internalize a belief that what was abnormal in a civilian setting was normal in combat. Military psychiatrists believed that incidents in the combat setting would not produce any lasting problems, that "only very sustained stress of a duration that rarely occurred in Vietnam could cause breakdown." This, in turn, could be treated by a temporary removal from a combat setting. Bourne suggested that two other factors limited the incidence of recognizable stress breakdowns: widespread use of drugs to deflect symptoms and, as mentioned before, expeditious administrative discharges.[31]

However, within a few years after 1970 Bourne had uncovered disturbing new evidence of stress reactions among Vietnam combat veterans which were delayed until after the removal of the soldier from the combat setting or until his return to a civilian environment. The delayed reactions, said Bourne, were defensive adaptations to the "functionalist" ideology of combat which were inappropriate in non-combat or civilian surroundings. He traced manifestations of delayed stress to actual combat experiences, to ideological disillusionment, and to "shame and guilt fermented by public sentiment against the war in later years." Delayed stress occurred in many forms and in various degrees, but was often characterized by symptoms which precluded a successful entry by veterans into the mainstream of society. These symptoms included combat neuroses, severe and frequent moral crises, and readjustment problems such as drug abuse and chronic unemployment.[32]

The delayed stress phenomenon was referred to by clinicians and counselors variously as post-stress or post-Vietnam syndrome until the late 1970s, and was not recognized as a disorder outside the realm of standard personality malfunctions until the publication of the 1980 Diagnostic and Statistical Manual III (DSM III), a standard source of the psychiatric profession. According to DSM III, which re-named post-Vietnam syndrome "Post Traumatic Stress Disorder (PTSD),"the symptoms might become manifest both in veterans who had experienced acute combat reactions and in others, who did not begin to experience symptoms until long after leaving the combat situation. PTSD, reported DSM III, manifested itself in various "insidious processes," and often may have originally been diagnosed as an individual personality disorder such as schizophrenia or manic depression. Symptoms were commonly expressed in the form of painful recollections or nightmares, called flashbacks, during which the stressful event was re-experienced. The trauma of flashbacks generally led to "psychic numbing," or diminished responsiveness to external events. Veterans also experienced feelings of estrangement from one's pre-combat experiences and relationships. Furthermore, problems with personal intimacy and sexuality were common. In fact, Dr. Stephen Giles reported that the majority of veterans counseled at the Huntington Veterans Outreach Center were experiencing marital difficulties.[33]

The DEROS system contributed significantly to the nurturing of PTSD. While some of the advantages to DEROS were obvious, such as the assurance of a specific date on which the soldier would be free from the war, the disadvantages relative to PTSD did not begin to emerge until the mid-to-late 1970s. As mentioned previously, DEROS meant that the Vietnam experience became a solitary episode for each solider. The combat troop felt no continuity with those who preceded or followed him, or with others in his unit who also rotated on their own personal schedule. Consequently, the buffer which unit morale and cohesion created against combat stress in other wars was lost. Also, the Vietnam veteran returning home alone missed the opportunity World War II veterans had on the extended trip home as a unit. The "long boat ride" provided chances for the World War II combat soldiers to discuss and address combat experiences with their fellows, and establish a framework within which to handle the difficulties they experienced. When the Vietnam veteran returned to his community, his "DEROS fantasy" of leaving the war behind was commonly shattered almost immediately, as he encountered a confused, divided, and often hostile public.[34]

Of the 2.8 million American soldiers assigned to Southeast Asia from 1964-1973, nearly one million engaged in actual combat or were exposed to life-threatening situations. According to one conservative estimate, of the approximately 30,000 surviving Vietnam combat veterans living in the state of West Virginia, 7,000 suffer symptoms of PTSD. Often, these men and women have been reluctant to seek counseling or treatment, due largely to the "Appalachians' fear of health care workers and facilities: the complicated language, rigid time schedules, and uncertain explanations." A sense of stoic resignation in the face of misfortune is an adaptation to the physical and economic hardships of the region and to the traditional powerlessness of poor Appalachians. The numbing caused by exposure to trauma in Vietnam often does not produce "a great deal of concern in West Virginia," where it has commonly been attributed, by health care workers in the Veterans Administration as well as by family members, to "bad nerves."[35]

Appalachians, dependent on strong kinship ties for protection and reinforcement, have traditionally been suspicious of government bureaucracies, even though many develop strong loyalties to individual political figures. Suspicion of government authority, said Ernestine Thornton, deepened with the war in Vietnam. In addition, many from the area who served in Southeast Asia were poor and uneducated. She had "personal experience with soldiers who could not hardly sign their names," and were uncomfortable with the paperwork required to secure veterans' benefits. "Coming home to the type of treatment they received and the fact that they were being totally ignored by the VA," said Thornton, confirmed their mistrust.[36]

The VA offered little assistance to Vietnam veterans who experienced readjustment difficulties; few had anything of a positive nature to report on their contacts with the Veterans Administration. An ex-Marine voiced his bitterness with the VA:

> I've been back from Vietnam now for fifteen years. The VA never once knocked on my door and said, "What you need, bud, you got a problem?" And they're not going to. I'm not stupid. I see guys dying because of the insensitivity of our government. Dying because they can't feed their families, or because they've got a problem that our government needs to be dealing with. I know a guy that lives not two blocks from here that spent three months putting bodies in bags, shipping them home, as a

disciplinary action. After he spent nine months in the fucking field, okay? Ended up spending a year in prison down at Camp Lejeune, North Carolina, and this guy cannot get fucking PTSD [compensation from the VA]. He's got sixty pounds worth of psychiatric testimony that says he's got problems and has had 'em ever since he got back from Vietnam.[37]

The Veterans Administration is predominantly staffed by non-veteran civilians and veterans who represent the major established veterans organizations such as the Veterans of Foreign Wars. Max Cleland, a Vietnam veteran and triple amputee, was director of VA, however, during the Jimmy Carter administration. Cleland found that the prevailing attitude within the VA was that Vietnam veterans were "social misfits." Cleland's tenure at the VA was a frustrating time; VA employees saw the Agent Orange [dioxin exposure] and PTSD claims of Vietnam veterans as a "big hoax, like witchcraft." Cleland was an outsider to the VA establishment and compelled to fight for substance abuse and counseling programs for Vietnam veterans against advisers "wedded to old beliefs." Although Cleland guided several programs of benefit to Vietnam veterans to fruition, his term at VA has been termed a "draw."[38]

David Smythers of Kenova, West Virginia, was drafted into the Army even though he had a history of childhood nervous disorders. Smythers saw extremely heavy combat during his tour in Vietnam, including a siege at Khe Sanh which lasted nearly six weeks. Smythers was diagnosed as having PTSD; the VA, however, refused compensation on the grounds that his nervous problems were the result of a pre-existing condition. Khe Sanh, said Smythers, "just about destroyed me . . . . Can you imagine day and might treatin' you like a machine instead of a human being? I didn't feel like there was any excuse for the way we were gettin' done." Smythers has been plagued by combat nightmares to the point where he "was afraid to go to sleep anymore" and remains unable to hold a job. He angrily affirmed that "they [the VA] say I can work when I absolutely know that I can't. If it wasn't for HUD and food stamps, we'd be on the streets." Smythers claimed that many other Vietnam veterans are in a similar situation. "You have to have an arm or a leg off or somethin' before you can do any good. And they're turnin' down everybody. They're told by somebody to deny everybody." Smythers believed that Vietnam veterans had been "shortchanged" by the government and by the American people:

They were there when we asked them to go and they did it, they did it for a cause. It was a waste to begin with; it was a waste of money, machines, and human beings, but they still did it. Why turn your back on 'em, when they need it? It kind of reminds you like we was done like slaves. It was like the guns were more important than the humans, than our value, than our health.[39]

Gralen Hobble, a Virginian who grew up near the western Pennsylvania coalfields, remembered his tour in Vietnam as being one of almost constant combat. "We went out [on patrol] all the time; we'd go out like 60-80 days at at time." Hobble was "in battle since the first day we got there, the worst firefight I had the whole time I was over there, it lasted like seven days." Hobble was wounded by a land mine after six-months in Vietnam. His injuries were aggravated when one of the straps holding his body onto the runners of an evacuation helicopter broke. As he was Medevaced, Hobble's legs were dangling from the helicopter and banging into tree branches. During surgery for stomach wounds at the VA Hospital in St. Albans, New York, doctors left a wire clip in Hobble's intestine. Years later when he reported stomach pains which "doubled him over," a VA physician told Hobble the pain was in his head, not his stomach. "It can't all be in my head," Hobble told the doctor. "I sure don't *want* to be sick. So I just got discouraged with them and walked out." Hobble picked shards of metal from his midriff for years as pieces of the clip surfaced. While at St. Albans recovering from his battle wounds, Hobble had undergone drug therapy, treatment common to returned combat veterans in some VA facilities:

They kept me on morphine and it was great, got rid of the pain and everything, but the thing was, I just felt like a stump. I wasn't doing nothing, I wasn't taking care of myself; I felt like I was gonna' get hooked on it or something . . . you had no control over your body. I told 'em they had to take me off of it 'cause I just couldn't handle it no more. [Morphine] made my body feel good, but my mind just wasn't all there.

I was just laying in bed and the next thing I knew it was night-time again. I just told the doctor I refused to take it. They took me off [morphine] and they give me real strong Darvons. It got to the point where I didn't really want to take them . . . so I just stashed 'em.[40]

Doug Johnson met similar frustrations when he sought medical attention through the VA. Johnson began experiencing the symptoms of PTSD approximately two-and-a-half years after he returned to Huntington from Vietnam. He encountered skepticism at the Huntington VA Hospital and in local mental health facilities when he sought counseling for his problems. "I did not socialize one-to-one," said Johnson. "I couldn't handle it. I didn't have the foundation to be able to date anybody. And the few people who would date us, figured we were all into drugs and bein' crazy. People were [more] willing to accept us as long as we acted crazy." Johnson began taking classes at Marshall University in 1968, but felt "very isolated. I would try to talk about things with people but once people found out a lot of guys were Vietnam vets, they either ignored us or asked the three famous questions: 'How was the dope? Did you kill anybody? How was the [sex]?'" Johnson remembered that the Vietnam veterans on Marshall's campus kept to themselves:

> Most of my friends were Vietnam veterans. It was the only way we were able to relate. I think all of us tried, people were just not willing to accept us. About the second semester 1969, I started comin' apart, real slow. Everybody would walk around it [when he went for counseling]; nobody wanted to talk about [the war]. They didn't know anything; nobody was willing to learn. I'd have these horrible combat dreams. I dreamed the same dream regarding those four children I killed for over ten years. Every time I would start [the doctors] would shut me up; not one of those bastards wanted to talk about Vietnam. VA hospitals wouldn't touch me.[41]

The VA hospitals, said Johnson, employed very few Vietnam combat veterans. "I don't think a lot of people can really get a handle on the way these guys are feelin'," said Johnson. "Unless you've been there, you're not really going to know." Drug treatment for "stressed out" veterans, said Johnson, was widespread and inconsistent at the VA. "If the guy's too upset or he seems to be particularly violent or nasty, zap him with medication." Johnson believed the VA was abrogating its duty to the veterans by depending on drugs as therapy, and leading them to dangerous chemical dependencies. "How the hell [could] we have a problem to deal with when you got us doped up? That doesn't make the problem go away, it just means that we can't begin to deal with it." Johnson, and some other West Virginia Vietnam veterans, have traced their experiences with PTSD by referring to their college transcripts. When the symptoms were overt, Johnson explained, his grades suffered noticeably because he could not concentrate in class. "I would get flashbacks," he recalled. "It would get so bad I couldn't even walk across the campus without gettin' one big flashback and staying' in it for an hour." Nobody at this stage [early 1970s], said Johnson, was willing to focus on the possibility that many of his symptoms were related to his experiences in Vietnam.[42]

The readjustment problems encountered by Vietnam veterans were not limited to emotional and medical matters. The damage to the generation's ideals about America's status as a just nation extended to the erosion of the country's economic promise and the open arms with which a strong economy had traditionally welcomed its returning warriors. Vietnam veterans came home to an economy in recession, and this hit Appalachia particularly hard. "While we were in Vietnam serving," said John Williams, "our peers were over here getting educations, landing the better jobs, and there really wasn't much left for us when we got back because the economy swung the other direction over the years." Because they "were supposed to be the drug crazed murderers of the twentieth century," veterans such as Williams faced a definite social prejudice, which further limited their employment options.[43] A Hurricane, West Virginia veteran believed the lack of employment opportunities was perhaps the key element in the instances of Post Traumatic Stress Disorder:

> The Vietnam veteran came back to a characteristically unwelcom[ing] society, high unemployment, which I think probably feeds what might have been a fuse within a lot of these guys. They were angry, most of them came back wanting to get back in the mainstream of society and were accustomed to having a role and objective and just going on with your life; when they hit the streets back here, they couldn't pick up where they left off . . . the combination of stress and having a family and not being able to feed them, not being able to meet society's opinion of a man; I think if there had been a better employment rate or more opportunities when they came back, I don't think there would have been this stress we see now.[44]

Faced with emerging public awareness of the neglect of Vietnam veterans, the United States Government was compelled to take some action to address that neglect. In 1979, largely as a result of lobbying by the newly organized Vietnam Veterans of

America and the efforts of the Vietnam Veterans in Congress caucus, the United States Congress enacted legislation to establish Readjustment Counseling Centers for Vietnam veterans around the country. These "storefront" counseling programs were funded through the Veterans Administration but were not designed to operate within VA facilities. The Veterans Centers represent a relatively informal atmosphere where Vietnam veterans meet with counselors and other veterans, individually or in group "rap sessions," to talk about their experiences and attempt to work out continuing readjustment problems. The Centers have made significant progress in their outreach to Vietnam veterans, but have been under constant attack from the Reagan administration. The next chapter will explore the establishment of the Veterans Centers and assess their impact on the readjustment of regional Vietnam veterans.

# Notes, Chapter III

[1]Paul Camacho, "From War Hero to Criminal: The negative Privilege of the Vietnam Veteran" in Figley and Leventman, *Strangers at Home*, p. 268. Jonathan Schell, *The Time of Illusion* (New York: Praeger, 1980), p. 8.

[2]Camacho, p. 268. Camacho said the administrations of Johnson and Nixon did this primarily by means of "media events," notably the trial of Lieutenant William Calley for the May Lai massacre and shifting blame for covert operations, such as surveillance of private citizens, to the Army when other agencies were more heavily involved.

[3]Ibid, pp. 268-69. Interview with David Evans, Charleston, West Virginia, November 10, 1984.

[4]David M. Bonior, Steven M. Champlin, Timothy S. Kolly, *The Vietnam Veteran: A History of Neglect*, (New York: Praeger, 1984), p. 107. The categories for discharges are Honorable, General, Undesirable, Bad Conduct, and Dishonorable.

[5]John P. Wilson, quoted in Jim Goodwin, *Continuing Readjustment Problems Among Vietnam Veterans: The Etiology of Combat Related Post Traumatic Stress Disorder* (Cincinnati, Ohio: Disabled American Veterans Press, 1984), p. 11; Evans interview.

[6]Bonior, *A History of Neglect*, p. 109.

[7]Charleston *Daily-Mail*, May 14, 1979.

[8]Charleston *Daily-Mail*, January 28, 1981.

[9]Huntington *Herald-Dispatch*, May 24, 1980.

[10]Camacho, "From War Hero to Criminal," p. 271.

[11]Charleston *Gazette-Mail*, November 11, 1984.

[12]Interview with Bill Fox, Huntington, West Virginia, November 17, 1984.

[13]Ibid.

<sup></sup>

<sup>14</sup>Interview with Jeff Payne, Hurricane, West Virginia, October 16, 1984.

<sup>15</sup>Ibid.

<sup>16</sup>Interview with Glen Hager, Huntington, West Virginia, September 17, 1984.

<sup>17</sup>Ibid.

<sup>18</sup>Interview with Ernestine Thornton, Charleston, West Virginia, November 21, 1984.

<sup>19</sup>Interview with John Williams, Huntington, West Virginia, October 13, 1984.

<sup>20</sup>Ibid.

<sup>21</sup>Ibid. Williams has since completed a BA in English at Marshall.

<sup>22</sup>Walter Capps, *The Unfinished War: Vietnam and the American Conscience* (Boston: Beacon Press, 1982), p. 89.

<sup>23</sup>Lawrence M. Baskir and William A. Strauss, *Chance and Circumstance: The Draft, the War, and the Vietnam Generation* (New York: Alfred A. Knopf, 1978), pp. 149-50.

<sup>24</sup>Ibid., p. 151.

<sup>25</sup>Interview with David Addlestone, Washington, D. C., August 8, 1985. Baskir and Strauss, *Chance and Circumstance*, p. 144.

<sup>26</sup>Interview with Mark Moore, Huntington, West Virginia, September 24, 1984.

<sup>27</sup>Baskir and Strauss, *Chance and Circumstance*, p. 147.

<sup>28</sup>Interview with Rich Richards, Charleston, West Virginia, November 10, 1984. Evans interview.

<sup>29</sup>Fox interview. Interview with Doug Johnson, Huntington, West Virginia, June 4, 1986. Bonior, *A History of Neglect*, pp. 39-40. Baskir and Strauss recounted an episode of "Hawaii Five-O"

when, after a drug related homicide, the Five-O detectives were ordered to run a check on all the Vietnam veterans in the area. *Chance and Circumstance*, p. 47.

[30]Daniel Sumrok, Steven L. Giles, and Mildred Mitchell-Bateman, "Public Health Legacy of the Vietnam War: Post Traumatic Stress disorder and Implications for West Virginians," *The West Virginia Medical Journal* 79 (September, 1983), p. 191.

[31]Peter Bourne, quoted in Robert F. Pazzerella, "Psychiatric Syndromes, Self-concepts, and Vietnam Veterans" in Charles R. Figley, ed. *Stress Disorders Among Vietnam Veterans: Theory, Research and Treatment* (New York: Brunner/Mazel, Publishers, 1978), p. 148.

[32]IBid., p. 149.

[33]Sumrok, Giles, and Mitchell-Bateman, *Public Health Legacy*, pp. 192-83.

[34]Ibid., p. 193.

[35]Ibid., p. 197.

[36]Interview with Ernestine Thornton, Charleston, West Virginia, February 7, 1986.

[37]Richards interview.

[38]Bonior, *A History of Neglect*, p. 169.

[39]Interview with David Smythers, Kenova, West Virginia, April 3, 1985.

[40]Interview with Gralen Hobble, Charlottesville, Virginia, November 24, 1984.

[41]Johnson interview.

[42]Johnson interview. Interview with Roger Sanford, Huntington, West Virginia, September 11, 1984. Hager interview.

[43]Williams interview.

[44]Payne interview, October 16, 1984.

# Out of the Closet: Veterans Outreach and Early Organization by West Virginia Vietnam Veterans

The people of West Virginia were dramatically confronted with the frustration endured by many Vietnam veterans on October 21, 1979 when a distraught Vietnam combat veteran named Harold Mann burst into the St. Albans, West Virginia Church of Christ armed with a 7 mm rifle. The Mann incident captured the attention of the nation, and for the first time familiarized many West Virginians with the terminology and manifestations of Post Traumatic Stress Disorder. Harold Mann symbolized the bitterness which underlay the return home of the veterans and his actions appeared to generate some positive public response to the neglect with which Mann and others had been treated. Significantly, the Mann episode also encouraged other local veterans to speak out and to begin to organize politically.

Harold Mann had been an ambulance driver in Vietnam. Psychiatrists who later examined him agreed that his desperate action in the St. Albans church was triggered by mental problems associated with his tour in Vietnam and his subsequent frustration with the Veterans Administration. Mann's pleas for treatment for debilitating headaches, which he attributed to his tour of duty, were turned down repeatedly by the VA. For over three hours Mann held hostage fifteen members of the congregation and several reporters, all of whom were released unharmed after he was allowed to issue a statement over WCHS (Charleston) radio. Mann's short statement, laced with profanity, warned the residents of the Kanawha Valley to be aware of the readjustment difficulties of many combat veterans and a warning to "stop some of the . . . kids from going to fight the next war for these son of a bitches [war profiteers] so they can make a . . . fortune." Mann, expressing a resentment common to many veterans who came home to high unemployment, angrily denounced the "draft dodgers" who had returned to the United States under President Carter's amnesty program and found work. Mann reflected the frustration of veterans who bore the burden of proving to the VA that their symptoms were service connected. He claimed that the VA dismissed his emotional and physical suffering as something "you just have to live with" and offered treatment only with a variety of drugs. "They [the government] didn't try a goddamn thing to do anything for you.

And once the war was over they didn't give a goddamn about any of our veterans anymore."[1]

On October 25 the Charleston *Gazette*, responding editorially to the Mann incident, declared that Vietnam veterans indeed had "a right to be bitter." Justifying the intervention in Vietnam proved to be difficult, said the editor, and in the final analysis impossible. Those who fought were drawn largely from those lowest on the economic and education ladder, who for "ill-defined reasons were sent to wage the cruelest kind of war in a land with whose name they were unfamiliar." When the survivors returned, they observed business as usual in the country. The *Gazette* urged its readers to understand the "peculiar problems" of those the country had deliberately forgotten so as not to be reminded of the war, affirming that "they [the veterans], but not the nation, had gone to war. They were not heroes. They were a prominent part of a huge national embarrassment . . . ."[2]

Many readers of the *Gazette*, which reprinted Mann's unedited statement, apparently were more upset over his language than by the desperation which caused him to take hostages. One reader commented that he could not understand how the paper could justify printing "such filth for the people to read." Were there no morals left in our country? Did we have to have such language printed in our decent papers?[3] Vietnam veterans, however, were quick to come to Mann's defense. One, James Rice of Huntington, accused the American people of "turning a cold shoulder" to returned Vietnam veterans. Rice believed America just wanted to forget the war, declaring "it was a bad experience for the whole country; we're a constant reminder of it." He also criticized Jimmy Carter for pardoning draft evaders but not deserters. "At least," Rice insisted, "they [deserters] tried to do their part. Maybe their nerves couldn't take it, but they tried." Another Huntington area veteran called Mann's act tragic but understandable, explaining that his own experiences had led to frustrations similar to Mann's. Although he was unable to secure private health insurance, this veteran refused to deal with the Veteran Administration's "insidious, bureaucratic red tape," having been treated carelessly by the VA in the past. "I'd just as soon die as go back to a Veterans' hospital," he wrote. "You get so doggone sick you just die or live with the agony. Or you do what this guy [Mann] did. Go off the deep end."[4]

Galvanized by Mann's actions, about one dozen Huntington area Vietnam veterans organized a group called the Vietnam Veterans Survivors Council, which later formed the nucleus of Huntington Chapter #61 of the Vietnam Veterans of America. One of the first actions taken by the Survivors Council was a march from St. Albans to the steps of the West Virginia Capitol in order to raise money to help Mann pay for private psychiatric counseling. When the marchers were not allowed to talk with Mann in the Kanawha County jail, they "jumped in the truck and drove up to see [Governor] Jay [Rockefeller]" at the governor's mansion. "The guards came out like we were gonna' take over the mansion," Doug Johnson remembered. The group's purpose was to persuade Rockefeller to intercede with the sheriff's office and allow Mann to see his family, which the sheriff later arranged. "My God," said Johnson, "even the maggots up at Moundsville [the state penitentiary] got more rights than Harold got." The members of the Survivors Council explained to the Charleston media that while they did not agree with the action Mann took, they believed it was "atrocious that he felt under the circumstances . . . like that's what he had to do. We're tryin' to get somebody in here to vouch for him and recognize that he has a legitimate problem." Johnson believed that Mann's outburst at the Church of Christ and the public awareness created by that act, together with the efforts of the Vietnam Veterans Survivors Council, provided much of the impetus for the establishment of the Veterans Readjustment Centers in Huntington and Charleston.[5]

At the time of the Mann episode, Malcolm Farmer, chief of counseling and rehabilitation services for the VA in Huntington, appeared reluctant to directly acknowledge pervasive readjustment problems among Vietnam veterans. Farmer reported that he had been "heartened" by the statistics on West Virginia Vietnam veterans. West Virginia, said Farmer, enjoyed a "rather unique" situation in that "the large number of unemployed just don't seem to exist in our state . . ." Farmer did acknowledge, however, the "strange syndrome" of delayed stress and attributed the VA's difficulty in assisting troubled veterans, "if we have one," to the reluctance of veterans to come out of the small rural areas to VA hospitals for counseling. He concluded that many Vietnam veterans' lack of trust in the government and its bureaucracy prevented them from approaching the VA for help. A vocational rehabilitation specialist at the Huntington VA, while affirming that the "overwhelming majority" of West Virginia Vietnam veterans had successfully re-entered the mainstream, acknowledged that "there are those who do feel rejected by society, who feel they were used. We're not seeing them, they're the ones we want to reach and help."[6]

*Operation Outreach*, authorized by Congress in the 1979 Health Care Amendments Act and funded through the Veterans Administration, was signed by President Jimmy Carter in June,

1979. In December of that year, less than two months after Harold Mann took hostages at the St. Albans Church of Christ, an Operation Outreach office opened in Charleston. In May, 1980, a more extensively staffed readjustment counseling center opened in Huntington. The center [hereafter the Vet Center], was opened as "a tangible symbol of a new public acceptance of the Vietnam veteran's dilemma."[7]

Myra MacPherson wrote in *Long Time Passing* that the purpose of the Vet Centers was to permit veterans to "talk through and exorcise" the past in order to get on with the present. For years, she said, there was no such refuge; the VA, with its "hassles and red tape and papers and long waits and doctors who couldn't understand . . . was just one more place to resent." Congress originally appropriated $12 million for 90 centers nationwide; by 1983, there were 135 centers funded at $21 million. By August, 1983, 200,000 veterans had sought out the services offered by the centers.[8]

These figures, however, reflected only a beginning in addressing the needs of Vietnam veterans. At the Huntington Vet Center, for example, counseling team leader Dr. Stephen Giles estimated that anywhere from 20% to 50% of the 30,000 West Virginia Vietnam veterans needed the services the center offered, and that statistical research had suggested that as of 1979 approximately 80% of Vietnam veterans had "never talked about the war. They've just tried to forget it." Giles noted that current events often triggered stress reactions, events such as the heroes' welcome bestowed on the American hostages who returned from Iran early in 1981, the type of homecoming denied the Vietnam veterans.[9]

Glen Hager joined the staff at the Huntington Vet Center in June, 1980, just a month after its opening. Between 1980 and 1984 Hager conducted a weekly group rap session at the center, one of the longest continuing sessions in the country. He estimated that the Huntington Vet Center had counseled approximately 3,000 area Vietnam veterans in its first four years of operation. The informality of the center, said Hager, and its detachment from the VA hospital facility, were important elements in overcoming the reluctance of many Vietnam veterans to turn to the national government. However, because "we were brought in as the bastard stepchild of the VA . . . forced on the VA [by director Max Cleland], the regional offices were opposed to us until they learned that we could help 'em out." The centers were operated by a mix of "maverick counselors" and mental health professionals with traditional clinical training. Some of the counselors did not fit easily into the clinical mold prescribed by the VA. While such counselors often established a good rapport with the veterans who came to the centers because of their unconventional approach, some unfortunately lacked the administrative abilities pleasing to the VA bureaucracy. "They [the counselors] made an effort not to be associated with the VA," said one veteran. The casual clothing style of the counselors, the location of the centers within the community, "that was deliberate. I still see it. People are real suspicious of the federal government." A Huntington veteran, one of Hager's rap group participants, declared that "those people at the Veterans Outreach Center, they did me a world of good. I was able to discuss a lot of things that I'd never been able to discuss. It was just like a big weight had been lifted off of me."[10]

During 1980 the relationship between the American public and Vietnam veterans appeared to change dramatically. National polls, for example, revealed strong public support for increased benefits for Vietnam veterans. Congress set aside land near the Lincoln Memorial for the Vietnam Veterans Memorial, and America appeared to be psychologically prepared to begin healing the wounds of the Vietnam era. On August 18, 1980, Republican presidential candidate Ronald Reagan appeared before the Veterans of Foreign Wars national convention, seeking the VFW's endorsement for his campaign. Portraying the Vietnam war as "in truth, a noble cause," in which the United States had tried to help "a small country, newly free from colonial rule . . . in establishing self-rule and the means of self-defense against a totalitarian neighbor bent on conquest," Reagan appealed to his VFW audience to recognize the courage and service of Vietnam veterans. "They fought as well and as bravely as any Americans have ever fought in any war," said Reagan. "They deserve our gratitude, our respect, and our continuing concern." Despite his stirring rhetoric, Reagan's first act as president was to impose a hiring freeze on the Vietnam Veterans Readjustment Counseling Program. His administration's first budget proposed the elimination of the program. Further, Reagan asked Congress to terminate other special outreach programs for Vietnam veterans, including a government employment program for disabled veterans.[11]

When David Stockman, President Reagan's first Director of the Office of Management and Budget, appeared before Congress to lobby for the cutbacks and eventual elimination of the counseling program, the response from the media and the public jolted Congress into defending the continued operation of the Vet Centers. Vietnam veterans were outraged that Stockman, who had been a draft-exempt divinity student at Harvard during the war and active in the antiwar movement, referred to the centers as a "dispensable expenditure." Stockman questioned whether Vietnam veterans had "special needs" which demanded attention, dismissing them as a "noisy interest group" which led the "general press and public to believe things that just weren't so." Stockman said Vietnam veterans could get any necessary counseling at the VA hospitals, ignoring the fact that the VA's admitted inability to handle the needs of Vietnam veterans led to the creation of the centers originally.[12]

While the Congress defended the centers, the staff and bureaucratic structure of the Vet Centers have gradually drifted into the sphere of the VA. Glen Hager attributed this partly to "burnout" among the original Vet Center employees. Counselors were overworked and underpaid and were prime burnout targets as they "relived the pain of their clients, attempted to contact deeply alienated" veterans who did not seek help, and had to handle psychological emergencies. Many counselors themselves have suffered their own stressful memories of Vietnam. When faced with a range of PTSD symptoms in clients, particularly in emergencies, the counselors' own psychic stress often increased. As one counselor said, "I've had to go on crisis intervention missions, and being a little crazy myself . . . it's been a crazy four years."[13] The attractiveness of the readjustment counseling program, said Glen Hager, was that it was "radical but could operate within the system . . . as time goes on, we are becoming more like the system, and that's something that's bothering me at this point:"

> I think when [Congress] passed the [1979 Health Care Amendments] bill they were gonna' give something to Vietnam vets and then snap it back and say 'we give you that program for rehabilitation purposes, to get [your] act together.' And when Stockman came in, we were on the chopping block.
>
> I think the pressure is being put on us to conform. If something gets old it has to take on traditions or die. In the future I see [the program] being inside the hospital territory; I see them looking for personnel already that are more robot types, VA middle-management types that fit the mold. [Original employees] are being replaced more and more by the smooth bureaucrat, non-Vietnam vet . . . . I can see that happening as each month passes.[14]

Despite the trend to budget cutbacks, the Charleston Vets Center organized a women's group early in 1982 to help women who were involved with troubled Vietnam veterans. One woman commented that her husband was "very restless ever since he came back from Vietnam. He was unhappy in his job, he was not happy with his family, not really happy with anything." Echoing a common sentiment among the families of returned veterans, she believed her husband's situation was unique until she attended the women's group. Another referred to the suspension of emotional development in late adolescence, mentioned earlier by John Wilson, at a period when many soldiers were serving in Vietnam.

> The average age of our soldiers was nineteen. They were put into this war on a one-to-one basis and that's the only way they know how to deal with things. I don't think my husband had the knowledge to cope with life then . . . .
> He had a best friend who was killed then. After that, he made friends but the men kept getting killed and pretty soon he didn't make any friends, didn't want to be hurt anymore, and it carried over into his later relationships with people.[15]

Her husband was 70% disabled and living on a retirement check, a "bothersome subject to him because he doesn't look disabled," and lived with guilt because he wasn't as badly hurt as others, "guilt that they fought, guilt that people think so badly of them and what they did over there." Before her husband began going to the Vet Center, she said, he had been in and out of VA hospitals, where he was treated mostly with medication, "to make him sleep." She referred to the VA as "an aggravation," unwilling to acknowledge the uniqueness of the Vietnam veterans' readjustment. "Did you know," she asked, "that more veterans have died since Vietnam than in Vietnam . . . by suicides, accidents, drownings? They can't cope with the stress. I don't think anyone is going to understand war unless they've been there."[16]

The Vet Center program, although it has strong defenders nationwide, has not escaped criticism even within the community of Vietnam veterans. Some centers were poorly run, said MacPherson; some counselors were on such ego trips that little was done for the clients seeking help. Some wives complained that their husbands were in worse condition after visiting a center, where they "reopened emotional wounds" which were improperly handled by inexpert counselors. One West Virginia veteran commented that he deliberately steered clear of the centers and rap sessions because "usually all you hear is how the government owes me money and . . . how Agent Orange ruined their lives and how other things have ruined their lives." All he believed society owed him was the opportunity to become a better citizen by financing his education, "which they are not willing to do. That's really my only complaint." Another believed that in some instances readjustment problems were used by veterans as a tool to "get away with a lot of anger, not to say they're not angry and have a reason to be . . . but I think it's overused. I choose not to attach that stigma to my life. I just choose not to be considered crazy and I'm sure as hell not going to go out there and put a big label on my forehead."[17] Still another consciously avoided seeking out other Vietnam veterans, although there were several in his circle of friends:

> I wasn't interested in joining anything. I don't particularly want to join anything. One friend suggested that there was a Vietnam veterans [rap group] of some kind active [here], and it had been very useful and very helpful for him to belong to it; guys who sit around and discuss war and . . . their own problems and readjustment and all that kinda' stuff. I didn't want to get involved in that, simply because I don't think I had any serious readjustment problems and don't want to sit around and listen to a bunch of people talk about how shitty life is; I'm not interested in that . . . . I am sympathetic, I know that there are some real problems. I don't think that I have any readjustment problems and actually, if I hang out in a group like that I might find out I do and I don't want to.[18]

At one time this veteran had been "totally unsympathetic" to others' accounts of readjustment difficulties. "I thought, if I can do it anybody can do it. They're all full of shit." But as time passed, he continued, he understood "more about what happened, the type of things that happened to people. I don't feel that way anymore. I'm more understanding."[19]

Overall, though some veterans and some of the American public have been ambivalent or hostile toward the centers and the idea of Vietnam veterans' "particular problems," the centers have filled a critical need in a neglected area. Their function, wrote MacPherson, was to make contact, to reach people others could nto reach. The centers produced "the same mysterious bonding that Alcoholics Anonymous has for people who went through years of psychiatry to no avail and then become faithful

AA converts." Part of their success has been the shift in public attitudes in the 1980s, permitting Vietnam veterans more latitude in discussing the war publicly and privately. "It's okay now to be a Vietnam veteran," said a Huntington veteran. "It's a bandwagon. It'll last for a while."[20]

The construction of the Vietnam Veterans Memorial in Washington and increased favorable response from the press and public probably have lessened PTSD symptoms in many veterans. Others, however, concluded that recent responses have been too little, too late. The years spent making slow progress in Vietnam veterans policy, wrote David Bonior, were years lost to the veterans themselves. For many discharged between 1965-69, for instance, the programs of 1975 or 1980 probably came too late to help them work through their readjustment problems. The important decisions in their lives had already been made. Beginning again was only a romantic option. "We were the generation that got bit," Ernestine Thornton explained. "Bit hard. Hurt badly." No amount of belated memorials, welcomes home and salutes, she continued, "is ever going to be enough." She referred to veterans who were emotionally scarred from fifteen years of unemployment and the frustration of dealing with the VA and the public. "Those fifteen years are lost to them and the future ain't very bright. For me, it ain't enough. All that ain't enough."[21] Other veterans concurred:

> I think a lot of the stress, as we get older, we hit a stage where we know we're not gonna' make it with the things we've set up for our lives; that's already happened to me. I'm not gonna' make it, and I know it. I have this terrible, terrible rage that I can never get rid of. I look at how far I've come, and all I've survived. If a few people had been just a little bit kinder, I coulda' got maybe just that little break a little bit earlier, what could I have accomplished? I'll never know that.[22]

Another veteran did not believe the belated acceptance of Vietnam veterans could ever counterbalance what went before. "The attitude seemed to be that the best thing to do with Vietnam veterans is just sweep 'em under the rug . . . if you ignored them long enough they'd go away." Most veterans did go away, he said, in one way or another. "You'll find most of 'em did, they're either dead now, or in prison, or insane . . . things like that. So most of 'em did . . . just sort of disappear from the scene." He believed that few surviving veterans of his age were able to function productively in society:

There are a lot of veterans that fought and fought over certain issues . . . unsuccessfully to the point where they've just given up and said "to hell with it." We're not going to get any recognition for what we've done, 'course they spent millions of dollars to build  some kind of a damn monument in Washington, D. C. for those unfortunate ones who died and never came home which are the very ones we can't do anything for, while they still continue to ignore the ones that are alive and . . . [there] could be a little somthing done to help us get back into society.

It's taken me several years to get my feet on the ground enough to come back and get an education and now . . . I'm going to be eliminated from the majority of employment opportunities. I'm just going to take what I get out of this life, that's all I can do now. Of course, time's running out on me.[23]

The desperate action by Harold Mann in the St. Albans Church of Christ dramatically revealed to West Virginians the bitterness and frustration characteristic of many Vietnam veterans who had become alienated from their ideals, their heritage, their government, and their people. Alienation was pervasive among Vietnam veterans, as many experienced a sense of betrayal in light of the deception inflicted upon them by the government and the neglect from the public. Some veterans attempted to overcome alienation by organizing politically to promote and ensure Vietnam veterans' rights and, to a degree, educate the public to the mechanism of policy which led the country into the Vietnam debacle. The most visible Vietnam veterans organization is Vietnam Veterans of America, Inc., formed in 1977 in Washington, D. C. The background, motivation, and organizational controversies involved in the formation and development of this advocacy organization, from national and local perspectives, demand separate treatment.

# Notes, Chapter IV

[1]Charleston *Gazette*, October 22, 1979, November 26, 1980.

[2]Charleston *Gazette*, October 25, 1979.

[3]Charleston *Gazette*, October 30, 1979.

[4]Charleston *Gazette*, October 24, 1979.

[5]Interview with Doug Johnson, Huntington, West Virginia, May 15, 1986. Charleston *Daily-Mail*, May 10, 1980.

[6]Charleston *Daily-Mail*, October 23, 1979; May 14, 1979; Charleston *Gazette*, October 24, 1979.

[7]Huntington *Herald-Dispatch*, May 24, 1980.

[8]Myra MacPherson, *Long Time Passing: Vietnam and the Haunted Generation* (New York: Doubleday and Company, 1984), p. 270.

[9]MacPherson, *Long Time Passing*, p. 270; Charleston *Daily-Mail*, July 2, 1980; Huntington *Herald-Dispatch*, May 24, 1980.

[10]Interview with Ernestine Thornton, Charleston, West Virginia, February 7, 1986; MacPherson, *Long Time Passing*, p. 271; Interview with Glen Hager, Huntington, West Virginia, September 17, 1984; Johnson interview.

[11]David M. Bonior, Steven M. Champlin, Timothy S. Kolly, *the Vietnam Veteran: A History of Neglect* (New York: Praeger, 1984), p.75.

[12]MacPherson, *Long Time Passing*, pp. 274-75.

[13]Hager interview. MacPherson, *Long Time Passing*, p. 274-75.

[14]MacPherson, *Long time Passing*, p. 271. Hager interview.

[15]Charleston *Daily-Mail*, March 3, 1982.

[16]Ibid.

<sup>17</sup>MacPherson, *Long Time Passing*, p. 271. Interview with John Williams, Huntington, West Virginia, October 13, 1984; Interview with Jeff Payne, Hurricane, West Virginia, October 16, 1984.

<sup>18</sup>Interview with Al Van Dyke, Charlottesville, Virginia, July 16, 1985.

<sup>19</sup>Ibid.

<sup>20</sup>MacPherson, *Long Time Passing*, pp. 271-72. Hager interview.

<sup>21</sup>MacPherson, *Long Time Passing*, p. 272. Bonior, *a History of Neglect*, p. 78; Thornton interview.

<sup>22</sup>Johnson interview.

<sup>23</sup>Williams interview.

# Those Who Organize: National and Local Perspectives on Development and Division Within the Vietnam Veterans of America

Vietnam veterans learned through bitter experience that traditional veterans organizations had little interest in welcoming the soldiers from the divisive Indochina war into their ranks. After confronting indifference or hostility from established veterans groups and the general public, some veterans of the Vietnam war began to transcend the individualization of their Vietnam experience and identify with their comrades in arms not only emotionally but politically. Convinced after years of neglect that the fair treatment of veterans had less to do with justice and morality than with political power, Vietnam veterans began to mobilize a veterans' rights movement in America. Because the genesis and fitful growth of the political organization of West Virginia Vietnam veterans has been closely related to the broader coalescence of the veterans nationally, it is necessary to outline the politicization of Vietnam veterans on the national as well as the state and local levels. The process of organization, roughly parallel nationally and in West Virginia, has been volatile.

The conflicts Vietnam veterans had with the Veterans Administration were exacerbated by the prevailing public perception of them. During the homecoming period for Vietnam veterans in the early 1970s the mass media played a significant role in the creation of a negative image of the veterans. News stories in particular emphasized the Vietnam veteran status of veterans involved in serious crimes. Police dramas on television furthered the negative image of the veterans, portraying them as "major antagonists, addicts, rapists, mass killers, and . . . morally offensive criminals."[1]

Even those who were advocates for Vietnam veterans often reinforced negative images. Many early psychiatric studies of the veterans were influenced by the antiwar sentiments of their authors. Veterans, therefore, were often portrayed as victims of the war, but also stereotypically as personally disorganized, beset with problems, and potentially dangerous. Clinicians learned that portraying Vietnam veterans as a "normal" group led to public apathy. Emphasizing the problems of veterans attracted more publicity but also supported commonly negative characterizations. In the public eye, "normal" was considered deviant for Vietnam veterans, while "pathology" was the expected norm. "Through this storm of speculation," one student of returned veterans concluded, "the Vietnam veteran continued to hide his identity and continued to endure . . . in spite of the American people."[2]

Because Vietnam veterans returned to America individually and anonymously rather than as a "coherent entity capable of collective action, they remained estranged from sources of political power" and were not often able to take effective action to combat the distorted image of them. Vietnam veterans were excluded from the traditional veterans lobby represented by the Veterans of Foreign Wars and the American Legion, often being alienated from the entrenched veterans organizations by generational, lifestyle, and political differences and by the reputation of losing the war. Returning to a recessionary economy and denied the educational opportunities of other veterans, Vietnam veterans grew to resemble a "prototypically estranged group, an ethnic minority such as American blacks who because of brutalization and alienation from their own original culture came to lack a fundamental self-pride, seeing themselves [negatively] through the eyes of [other Americans]." Lacking a cohesive lobbying organization, and with no political power base, Vietnam veterans were generally isolated from the power centers of American politics, and, therefore, were effectively disenfranchised.[3]

In order to combat the negative images of Vietnam veterans and to promote a positive agenda for their rights, many Vietnam veterans saw a need for a political organization. The process of organizing Vietnam veterans into an effective lobby was undertaken late in 1977 by a small group under the leadership of Robert O. Muller, a Marine infantry commander in Vietnam who was paralyzed from the waist down by enemy fire. *Washington Post* columnist Colman McCarthy noted the formation of Muller's group and the need for a Vietnam veterans' advocacy organization:

> The closed world of veterans affairs—the trinity of the VA, Congressional Committees, and traditional organizations like the American Legion, the Veterans of Foreign Wars, and the Disabled American Veterans—often created pacts of faint protection, at the expense of many [Vietnam era] veterans excluded from the decision-making process.[4]

Muller was well aware of the obstacles to forming a new veterans organization. Traditional veterans groups functioned not only to promote public consciousness of veterans' needs, but also to co-opt a potentially disruptive group, i.e., a new generation of veterans, so that they accepted rather than rejected the status quo within which the traditional groups functioned. Journalist James Ridgeway, who chronicled the development of VVA in several articles, commented in 1984 on the potentially progressive challenge Muller's organization could pose to the older, conservative veterans groups. Ridgeway noted that such a challenge was not without historical precedent. Immediately following the World Wars powerful new veterans' movements allied with the labor movement and other forces to promote veterans' rights. The World War Veterans and the Private Soldiers and Sailors Legion, in alliance with the Industrial Workers of the World and the Farmers' Non-Partisan League, challenged the American Legion between 1918 and 1923. The American Veterans' Committee vied with the Legion and the VFW for the allegiance of World War II veterans. Both movements, wrote historian Terry Radke, a student of left-wing veterans' organizations, attempted to "place the bread-and-butter issues of servicemen and servicewomen within a broader vision of reform and social justice." Both movements also, Radke continued, lost a war of attrition with the American Legion because of the Legion's economic power, its endorsement by the federal government, and the "Red Scares" of the 1920s and late 1940s.[5]

Muller was determined that his organization, originally named the Council of Vietnam Veterans, would not be assimilated into the larger veterans lobby but would create a strong independent lobby for Vietnam veterans. At a Washington, D. C. symposium in 1980, he explained that the Vietnam Veterans of America [hereafter VVA] existed to meet the needs of Vietnam veterans which were attributable to their military service. VVA hoped to provide, beyond assistance for veterans' particular needs, "a measure of recognition and appreciation for what their experiences were and still are." Beyond these goals, said Muller, VVA wanted to serve as a catalyst in "America's coming to terms with the war and its warriors."[6]

Vietnam Veterans of America has been surrounded by controversy since its inception, largely due to the statements and public profile of Muller and other members of the national leadership. Much of Muller's personal agenda for veterans in post-Vietnam America was formulated at the Kingsbridge VA hospital during his recuperation from chest and spinal cord injuries. At that Bronx, New York, facility he endured the shabby treatment many wounded veterans received. His ward at Kingsbridge was featured in a 1970 *Life* magazine photo essay which shocked the nation with its revelations about the treatment with which some of the wounded lived, treatment punctuated by the fact that by

1980, eight of Muller's mates on the spinal cord ward had committed suicide. Muller was hardly surprised by the suicides, but he was angry about it and resolved to create in the American people an awareness that the "country's leaders who sent the young to war had little concern about their postwar lives."[7]

Because he became a spokesman for his ward, conducted interviews for newspapers and appeared on television, Muller was approached by members of the Vietnam Veterans Against the War [VVAW] after the *Life* article and asked to represent them to the media. Muller, having once joined the Marines, like many Vietnam veterans was reluctant to join any organization. Nevertheless, he did represent the views of VVAW for the public record. Primarily through his contacts in VVAW, Muller evolved a corpus of opinion about Vietnam veterans which he later came to see as fundamentally misconceived, a misconception which has had important implications for the development and direction of Vietnam Veterans of America. "Every single Vietnam veteran that I knew was a member of VVAW," recalled Muller. "Everyone of my friends went through the antiwar process." Expecting the broad spectrum of Vietnam veterans to have an antiwar critique of Vietnam by virtue of their experience, Muller discovered he had erred in his assessment. "I realized . . . that my [antiwar] experience, which I thought was the predominant experience of Vietnam veterans in this country, is clearly the minority experience."[8]

Muller asserted that it was significant that VVAW was the only serious manifestation of a Vietnam veterans organization while the war was in progress and, briefly, after the war had ended. "The only public image that really took hold of the Vietnam veteran," said Muller, "was that which was formed by the impression of the VVAW. The 'ragtag army,' wearing the old utilities and uniforms." The VVAW, he said, comprised of men and women who were wary of a rigidly formalized structure, was "a meeting of anarchists." The Vietnam generation, said Muller, but even moreso the Vietnam veterans themselves, had "strong feelings of alienation," and were suspect of authority figures; consequently, hierarchical organizational alignments were generally avoided by the veterans. David Addlestone, legal advisor to the Vietnam Veterans of America, reaffirmed this position. The Vietnam veterans, including the membership of VVA, were "thin-skinned, distrustful of authority," both in government and within the VVA. Addlestone labeled this mistrust as "part of the Vietnam veteran baggage." A manifestation of this attitude surfaced when a Huntington veteran, periodically active in Huntington Chapter #61 of the

VVA, warned that many veterans might be reluctant to participate in an oral history project which was conducted under the auspices of a state institution. Many Vietnam veterans, he said, believed they had been used once already and had no desire to be used again.[10]

Muller concluded that a pervasive reluctance existed among the veterans to submit to structure, discipline, and most organizational requirements. This reluctance was evident in VVAW and carried over to VVA. The VVAW, if atypically loosely structured among veterans groups, nevertheless was broadly-based and "to the extent that there was any public expression of Vietnam veteran sentiment it was clearly [through] VVAW." Muller cited the VVAW Winter Soldier Hearings in Detroit in 1971, documenting atrocities committed by American troops in Vietnam, demonstrations in Washington where combat medals were thrown onto the Capitol steps by protesting veterans, and the occupation of the Statue of Liberty by VVAW members, as incidents which set the VVAW image in the public perception. Although the Nixon administration publicly derided the VVAW-Vice-President Spiro Agnew called them "home front snipers," and the Nixon White House put together a "truth squad" called Vietnam Veterans For A Just Peace to counteract the public statements of VVAW-the news media were drawn to VVAW. VVAW, said Muller, offered "credentialing" to the peace movement. "We had spokesmen that [sic] paid their dues in combat," Muller said, "and had proven themselves to be willing to fight for America, and gave very compelling accounts of what they did in Vietnam and what they saw." But the "ragtag" image of VVAW, he continued, contributed to the perception by the World War II generation, particularly the veterans organizations, of Vietnam veterans as "being part of that longhaired, pot-smoking hippie generation that didn't fight the war as hard as they should have and lost."[11]

Although the older veterans organizations were open to Vietnam veterans for membership, and currently Vietnam veterans are heavily recruited by the aging Veterans of Foreign Wars, few Vietnam veterans until recently held leadership positions in them. But Muller's analysis of the misunderstanding between older veterans and the Vietnam veterans touched an issue for deeper than a generational gap. Beyond the competition for control of the veterans organizations, or the competition for federal money, there was a "fundamental division in the attitudes of younger and older veterans." The difference was especially reflected in the attitudes toward authority, particularly government. According to David Bonior, et al., Vietnam veterans, often uncertain of the war's meaning, shared in the national attitude of suspicion born of Vietnam and deepened by Watergate. The leadership of the older veterans organizations, wrote Bonior, seemed untouched by the war and the doubt it engendered. Bonior believed that the differences of older and younger veterans could have been defused had the major veterans groups cultivated Vietnam veterans in leadership positions. Those few who were in leadership roles were unable to offset policy, and were used to create a facade of Vietnam veteran support. For the younger veterans, this created a "leadership vacuum" in which their views and emotions went unspoken. Vietnam Veterans of America was created to fill this vacuum. VVA was conceived as a political advocacy organization, not, as a Charleston veteran said, as a "social club of drinkers, but an active organization fighting for the rights of veterans—not just Vietnam veterans but all [future] veterans."[12]

Robert Muller believed that the organization of Vietnam veterans into a positive lobby was essentially a political campaign, necessitating the education of his constituency concerning the nature of power relationships in America and how to direct those relationships into progressive, responsive government. Significantly, VVA's declaration of principles emphasized the mutual obligations between governors and governed, with "the latter recognizing an obligation of compulsory foreign or domestic service equitably shared by all, and the former morally obligated to implement foreign and domestic policies that are clear, consistent, and reflective of the will of the people." At the first VVA National Convention in Washington in 1983, the delegates passed a series of resolutions dealing directly with veterans issues and also with broader political concerns. The first resolution read "never again will one generation of veterans abandon another."[13]

The VVA has grown steadily, from the handful of original members in 1978 to about 30,000 members in November, 1985. That growth, however, has not come easily. For example, Muller re-financed his house to keep the organization solvent in 1979. However, by 1985, supported by dues, private contributions, and funds from the Combined Federal Campaign, a charity of federal government workers, VVA had an operating budget of $1,000,000 annually. With the organization's growth, however, has come continuous controversy.[14]

VVA gained national recognition late in 1981 when Muller led the first of several VVA delegations back to Southeast Asia to meet with Vietnamese officials for discussions about dioxin contamination, the results of the widespread American use of the defoliant Agent Orange during the first several years of America's involvement in the war. Also on the agenda were discussions focusing on Amerasian children and American soldiers missing in action. The delegation received promises of cooperation from the Vietnamese communist government on the search for MIAs and measuring the effects of Agent Orange on humans. The major story that came out of the visit, however, and which was latched onto by the media and the public, was the result of a symbolic incident. While in Hanoi, in line with the protocol for visiting dignitaries, the VVA representatives laid a wreath at the tomb of Ho Chi Minh which read "With Respect from the Vietnam Veterans of America." This, together with a visit to an American war crimes museum, touched a sensitive nerve among many Vietnam veterans in the United States.[15]

At a press conference shortly after the delegation returned from Vietnam, Muller and the others were denounced as communist dupes by two prominent Vietnam veterans. Frank McCarthy, co-founder of Agent Orange Victims International, called the delegation members "frauds" who had "betrayed every Vietnam veteran in this country." Al Santoli, a reporter for the *National Veterans Review*, criticized the VVA delegates for laying the wreath at Ho's tomb, calling them a "total disgrace to every one of us who served in Vietnam."[16]

The controversy over the visit to Ho's tomb has moderated over the past years but has continued to plague Muller and the VVA, particularly the national leadership. The furor caused by the visit divided Appalachian Vietnam veterans. While mindful of the serious need for a Vietnam veterans lobby, some were alienated by the apparent persistence of VVAW radicalism within the ranks of VVA. The controversy resurfaced in West Virginia in 1984, when National VFW Commander-in-Chief Clifford Olson chastised Muller and the VVA as "communist tools." Speaking at the VFW's Southern Conference in Charleston, Olson urged the United States Congress to deny a federal charter to VVA, a charter which would signify recognition by the government of the organization as a legitimate national veterans lobby. Olson, a Korean War veteran eager to attract Vietnam veterans into the ranks of his aging organization, was careful to make a distinction between VVA's national leaders and its local membership. Local chapters, said Olson, were doing a "fantastic job" counseling veterans and working on Agent Orange and benefits issues. Although he was convinced of the patriotism of VVA members in the coal country and heartland of America, Olson declared he could not support a national charter for VVA unless there was a change in the national leadership. Muller's visits in Hanoi-a second delegation went in 1983—"leave us wondering what his motives are . . . . There's no way on God's green earth [Vietnam veterans] have respect for Ho Chi Minh. [VVA leaders] are nothing more than a communist tool, used and propogandized." The 1981 visit to the war crimes museum further discredited Muller and his organization, said Olson. "These are the things that stick in your craw," he announced. "The U. S. didn't commit any war crimes . . . . I think he's knowingly being duped."[17]

Olson was probably taken aback by the responses his statements drew from the local VVA leadership in Charleston. West Virginia State Council president Dave Evans expressed resentment at Olson's attack on the leadership and Charleston surgeon Jim Rogers, a member of the national VVA board of directors, encouraged Olson publicly to reverse his position opposing the VVA charter. Olson reiterated that he was speaking only of the national leadership and refused to retract his comments. "In no way did I call these local people communists," said Olson. "I never once said anyone was a communist."[18]

The persistent bitterness over the wreath incident bespoke the political divisiveness which has permeated the Vietnam Veterans of America, posing a constant threat to the stability of the organization. A 1985 Louis Harris *Vietnam Poll of the General Population* documented what VA members such as Muller nationally and Evans and Rogers locally had reluctantly come to assume: support for the United States war effort in Vietnam was far more widespread among the veterans of the war than the founders of VVA had supposed. For a veterans advocacy organization born largely of the antiwar sentiment and sophisticated political critique of antiwar activists like Muller and Evans, the ambivalence of Vietnam veterans about the war and its conduct created significant challenges. To illustrate, 59% of Vietnam combat veterans polled answered affirmatively to the question "Do you feel you have a clear idea of what the Vietnam war was all about, that is, what we were fighting for?" Forty-six percent responded affirmatively to the question "Should we have become involved militarily in Vietnam?," while 45% answered negatively and 9% had no opinion. Robert Muller, convinced that America's involvement in Vietnam was orchestrated by military and political leaders with little or no interest in the well-being of the nation's soldiers or democratic institutions, was disturbed by these figures:

If we haven't [in the veterans community] come to a
consensus on where [the American people] failed, it's safe

to assume that a lot of the things that should be done to rehabilitate the decision-making process haven't been done because [we] don't agree on where the system fell apart. The whole mechanism which gave us Vietnam is essentially in place, to give us another problem.[19]

VVA legal advisor David Addlestone, who served a tour of duty in Vietnam and later returned to defend American military personnel there facing court martial, reported that, particularly in light of subsequent knowledge about Vietnam veterans' heterogeneous political formulations, the critical first return trip to Vietnam was improperly handled. Still a fledgling organization in 1981, VVA did not have the necessary outreach resources to brief its membership about the actual and symbolic purposes of the visit, which included dialogue on the promotion of diplomatic relations between the U. S. and the government of Vietnam, in addition to the POW/MIA, Amerasian children, and Agent Orange issues. The American press, said Addlestone, misinterpreted the purpose of the visit to Ho Chi Minh's tomb, and the weakness of the lines of communication between the national office and the grassroots membership prevented the national from adequately articulating "where the organization was headed."[20]

Jim Rogers of Charleston agreed. Rogers, who along with David Evans participated in a VVA delegation to Vietnam and Kampuchea in November, 1984, said much of the local leadership of VVA was concerned over Muller "doing things like laying a wreath at the tomb of Ho Chi Minh." This concern caused public relations problems in the veterans community and led to the fear among some of the West Virginia membership that the national leadership would go "too far to the left." There developed a concomitant fear within the national leadership that the mass membership could seize control of the organization and take it too far to the right. When Santoli and McCarthy attended the December, 1981 press conference "with the deliberate intention of attacking Bob Muller," said Rogers, "*that* became *the story* of the first visit back." The resultant "major controversy among Vietnam vets . . . probably . . . retarded the growth of the VVA." The fighting on the battlefield was over, said Rogers and the delegations were an attempt by VVA to recognize that publically and "get on with a positive agenda." The negative publicity, however, inhibited the rapid organization of a constituency wrestling with putting the war behind itself. The furor over the wreath incident "gave ammunition to those who didn't want to see any kind of Vietnam veterans organization, including some [of the] leadership of other veterans organizations." The Vietnam war was very divisive, and "to have an organization of Vietnam veterans [was] to remind the American people of the divisiveness of the Vietnam war, and to carry that into the future."[21]

The divisiveness of which Rogers spoke permeated VVA at all levels. Many West Virginia Vietnam veterans were far removed from the activist political agenda which the national organization followed, and raised questions about following the lead of national representatives who apparently had close associations with the veterans' recent enemies. At least one West Virginia VVA local was badly split by the Hanoi visit. Charleston Chapter #38 of VVA was formed in October, 1981, at a meeting in St. John's Episcopal Church on Quarrier Street. James Hill was elected #38's first president. Initially optimistic about the political direction upon which the chapter embarked, Hill soon became frustrated with the ideological factionalism within #38 and became less and less active in the organization. Hill perceived a "left wing" movement in the Charleston local. He withdrew from the presidency and was succeeded by Jim Rogers, who served as president from January, 1982 until July, 1983. Hill alluded to power politics within the chapter:

It was quite rigged for the present brand of leadership that they now have [1984], and they're all left wing, I will not say they're communist, I will not say they're socialist, they are left, and they have a very small membership because of all the hardcore left-wing radicals . . . . We [the right] have given up our membership and it is generally looked at as being kind of a radical organization to the left all the way to the top. You remember, the president of VVA is the one who laid the wreath on Ho Chi Minh's tomb in Hanoi, and it seemed he [Muller] was pampered down there.[22]

The "left wing" of which Hill spoke directed Chapter #38 towards an activist political agenda and cultivated a sophisticated and direct method of reaching the public, using visible demonstrations and maintaining a high profile in the local media. To facilitate communication between other VVA locals in West Virginia and to formulate a political agenda to present to the state legislature, the West Virginia State Council was formed in 1982, with David Evans as its first president.[23] Evans, who like Muller got involved in antiwar work with Vietnam Veterans Against the War, was determined to erase the "counterculture" stereotype of activist veterans while maintaining a progressive social and political program. VVAW was a good organization, said Evans, but "you can't be an anarchist and get things done . . . 'cause people will look at you as nothing more than an anarchist and loud-mouthed son-of-a-bitch." Evans pointed to the example of John Kerry, U. S. Senator from Massachusetts, who had been active with VVAW. "We got to be good friends [in VVAW]," said Evans. "And it's funny because he came from the same background I did; he was a loud-mouthed antiwar activist . . . a very militant protester . . . . He cleaned up his act up [sic] to the point where he took off the fatigues and put on the suit . . . the message is the same, but it's the appearance [which changed.]" Evans and Rick Richards recalled doing an interview  on the State Council with a Charleston newspaper reporter who pleaded with them to wear jungle fatigues for a photograph. They refused, and the refusal "kind of blew her away. We don't own any fatigues," they told her, whereupon the reporter offered to buy fatigues for them to wear. Evans and Richards were adamant. Part of their task with VVA was "to kill that image of the stereotyping we got from the media and the government."[24]

The State Council, which is comprised of delegates from each VVA chapter in the state, was organized partly to further distance Vietnam veterans from the negative image. The council was also established to serve as "more or less a governmental organization for the state chapters." The representatives determined an agenda and coordinated that through Richards, the Council's legislative affairs director. A key component of the State Council's purpose was familiarizing the statewide membership with public speaking. "That's something that Vietnam vets have never done," said Evans. "They're kind of backwards about joining and they've got some good ideas but you get 'em on camera . . . or in an interview and reporters tend to fuck them a little bit." Each State Council representative, said Evans, had practiced dealing with the press to the point where ". . . you walk up and stick a microphone in his face he can stand up to you and give you a hell of an interview and be very clear about what he wants to say." As far as political activism among West Virginia veterans of *any* era, said Evans, "this is the only thing going. This is it. This is the most politically oriented organization in this state . . . the Vietnam Veterans of America. The only way we can be successful in getting what we need," he continued, "is get it from the government. We realized that in 1978 [1977] when the organization was founded. You gotta' go to the source . . . . We can stand out and burn flags and throw bricks through windows for a week and they [politicians] won't notice." Rick Richards concurred. Throwing medals away wouldn't get one new bed in a VA hospital, he said. "But we can put on a suit and walk up to the legislature," Evans rejoined, "and kick ass."[25]

Evans, who was appointed by Muller to chair the VVA Select Committee on Governmental Affairs in 1983, and Jim Rogers formed part of the West Virginia delegation to VVA's first national convention in Washington, D. C., where Rogers was elected to his first term on the organization's National Board of Directors. One of the resolutions passed at the Washington convention authorized VVA's board to speak out on a wide range of foreign and domestic issues. "We've got to be first and foremost a veterans service organization," Evans explained, "but we can't neglect the broader issues of economics, foreign policy, health care, or anything else that affects us, as veterans or people. We're not trying to be the conscience of the American people," he continued, "but we would like to share our experience about what the hell you can get into when you get into a war."[26]

The West Virginia State Council capitalized on the convention's admonition to speak out on social issues, endorsing humanitarian aid to the government of Vietnam and calling on all Vietnam veterans to mobilize opposition to American military involvement in Central America. In fact, Chapter #38 issued a declaration of anti-intervention in El Salvador in 1981, two years before a similar national VVA resolution was passed. "We did it on the steps of the State Capitol," said Evans, "when the legislature was in session. We had more press than we could handle. We had to do the damn thing twice."[27]

Evans's sense of having a political role to play was heightened by the deaths of American Marines in Lebanon and the Grenada invasion, as well as by contact with Marine recruits, whom he found to be "just as naive and gung-ho [about war] as I was when I was nineteen." Consequently, the West Virginia State Council issued a press release almost immediately after the October, 1983, bombing in Beirut which killed nearly 250 U. S. Marines:

[We] demand that President Reagan remove all U. S. forces from Lebanon at once . . . and that congress withdraw its support for the war as stated in the War Powers Act of 1973. This situation is currently a parallel of the incidents that led us into the war in the Republic of Vietnam.[28]

Within six hours of the bombing of the Marine barracks, Evans was in contact with each member of the State Council in order to draft the news release. Early on the morning of October 24, 1983, Evans appeared on Charleston television with the statement:

> Our national headquarters calls us [to ask] "How in the hell can you do stuff this quick?" Well, we did it. Roger Sanford and I had it typed up and delivered to the press. We were the only ones that said anything. The VFW failed to respond, either negatively or positively. The Vietnam Vets [sic] of America are caring enough to get out there and maybe take some flak and say "this is wrong." Who was responsible [for the Marines killed in Beirut]? Don't blame it on the Marine commander. Who sent them there?[29]

The 1983 convention in Washington marked a turning point for the Vietnam Veterans of America. The growth and strength of the organization, said Robert Muller, indicated that the American public was finally prepared to acknowledge the Vietnam veteran and "the Vietnam experience, and the veterans are finally ready to join together as a catalyst. We have become the vehicle to make a movement." Commenting on VVA's role as an unofficial liason between Washington and Hanoi, Muller said VVA expected to play "a critical role as a facilitator in the discussions [primarily on MIA] to insure the talks continue on an aggressive basis." Delegates to the convention passed more than eighty resolutions, on issues such as broad political and social organizational involvement, Agent Orange research, normalization of relations with the Vietnamese government, MIAs, and foreign policy. Evans's Governmental Affairs Committee declared its intention to formulate VVA policy statements in the areas of human rights, social and economic justice, foreign policy, and military strength. A Governmental Affairs resolution on compulsory military service stated that, whereas Vietnam veterans were mindful of "traditional inequities in the draft laws and their administration during the Vietnam War," any future draft must be equitable "in that a fair cross-section of American society irrespective of either sex, sexual preference [or] social and economic position, be represented in our Armed Forces."[30] The delegates also approved a resolution opposing U. S. military intervention in Central America until a "clear sense of public support for our mission there" developed. And, Robert Muller affirmed, despite the growth of the organization, the VVA "won't shed the activist image that often has irritated traditional veterans groups and the government."[31]

The West Virginia State Council continued to pursue the course encouraged by Muller, when in 1983-84 it successfully lobbied in the West Virginia state legislature. State Council legislative coordinator Rick Richards lobbied at the Statehouse for six specific pieces of legislation, all of which were passed, including a plan to facilitate the testing of West Virginia Vietnam veterans exposed to Agent Orange and a bill establishing low-interest housing loans for eligible veterans. Richards noted that Vietnam veterans received a fair hearing from the legislature, but expressed frustration at his dealings with the administration of Governor Jay Rockefeller, particularly the Department of Veterans Affairs and its director, Jack Moon. "When we get together with him [Moon]", said Richards, "he doesn't want to talk about veterans issues. He wants to tell me I have some bad habits. 'Rick, you have no class'. 'Jack, you're right. I have no class. Now, what the fuck are you gonna' do for the veterans that are blowing their brains out, out there?'."[32] Class or no class, the media and lobbying tactics of VVA led to positive legislative results. Part of those tactics included stylistic adaptations to the norms of typical lobbyists. Part included a degree of advocacy and confrontation unfamiliar to legislators dealing with veterans. "For years we had to face the crazed killer stereotype," said Evans. These days, our idea . . . is to show up in three-piece suits instead of jungle fatigues. I think it's helped change the public's perception of us." The polished image, however, belied an activism and irreverence born of th VVA leadership's combat experiences and subsequent ostracism, stripping away the deference to the lawmakers' powerful position which was customary among lobbyists:

> We don't go in there with this humble, hold you higher than God attitude. We go in like Jay Rockefeller or Jack Moon, or anybody in government is working for us. We go in like we own the damn place, 'cause we do. We bring in the media and that just blows their mind 'cause they've worked with other veterans organizations who've been complacent.[33]

The activist image Robert Muller vowed to retain at the first VVA National Convention, however, underwent some severe constraints at the national and state levels by the time of the second National Convention in Detroit, November, 1985. There, the VVA delegates passed an amendment to the constitution limiting the latitude of the national leadership and the State Councils relative to adopting policies or positions "with respect to matters involving foreign or domestic affairs unless such issues directly affect veterans affairs, or are issues of domestic concern related to the economic, physical, or emotional well-being of veterans." Local chapters were exempted from the restrictions of the amendment, being permitted to adopt policies on domestic or foreign issues upon affirmation by 2/3 of those members present at a duly constituted meeting.[34]

Passage of the amendment had the immediate effect of invalidating a number of resolutions which had previously been approved by the National Board, including resolutions attacking the Pentagon for promoting dangerous weapons systems, endorsing Congressional representation for the District of Columbia, and supporting "all efforts to impose economic sanctions, both public and private, against the government of the Republic of South Africa" for its perpetuation "of the intolerable form of oppression known as apartheid." Ironically, the amendment to limit VVA's participation in broadly based political, social, and economic affairs was sponsored by Robert Muller.[35]

Muller's reasoning for endorsing the limiting amendment was based upon two issues which threatened the future of his organization: the long and bitter struggle to secure Congressional approval for the VVA's National Charter, and Muller's growing fear, rooted in his critical initial misperception of the political attitudes of Vietnam veterans, that should the national leadership continue to speak out forcefully on social issues, the membership might remove them from office and replace them with a reactionary leadership.[36] At the first convention in Washington, although the delegates reiterated that VVA was first and foremost a veterans service organization, the leadership was allowed to address other matters. The "political formulation" of the VVA leadership, however, was unacceptable to "a certain spectrum of opinion in the U. S. Congress and the Reagan administration" which the VVA did not wish to alienate. Muller and the Board of Directors, over the objections of Jim Rogers, therefore, offered the amendment in order to appease their political opponents in the United States Senate (notably Jeremiah Denton of Alabama, a POW during the Vietnam War) who were blocking approval of the National Charter. The necessary two-thirds of the delegates passed the amendment.[37]

The West Virginia State Council assumed a more centrist position when Ernestine Thornton succeeded David Evans as president in June, 1985, becoming the first woman to lead a State

Council of the VVA. Although Thornton did not reveal how she voted on the limiting amendment at the Detroit convention, she offered her opinion as to the motivation behind it. "There's been a lot of criticism from . . . the more 'right-wing' faction of VVA regarding Muller and the national board's stand on international issues," said Thornton. "[The membership believed] 'if you're not speaking for all of us, maybe you shouldn't speak at all on certain issues'." Thornton attributed the widespread support of the amendment to a "maturing" of the organization, an accommodation to the give-and-take of politics. She believed Vietnam veterans perceived a need to direct their political energy more into veterans benefits concerns and less into broad social issues and foreign policy concerns. "We think more of ourselves. We don't have to address every single issue as a way to get attention drawn to us. We are learning to work within the system because the system is recognizing us."[38]

Whatever the power realities that lay behind Muller's sponsorship of the amendment, the initial results as far as consolidating the strength of Vietnam Veterans of America were substantial. Conditional upon approval of the amendment, for instance, the leadership of a small, conservative counter-organization to the VVA called the United Vietnam Veterans Organization merged with VVA, pushing the membership to over 30,000.[39] The amendment appeared to strike a theme of unity within the Vietnam veterans movement, according to Fred Donovan, editor of Charleston Chapter #38's newsletter, *The Guardian*:

> The convention endorsed Bobby Muller's call to make this an organization focused upon service, advocacy, and fraternity . . . .
> . . . . While Chapter #38's delegation initially opposed this restriction, we eventually were convinced that it was in the best interest of the organization and the Vietvet [sic] movement. Vietvet issues are too pressing to be sidetracked by foreign policy questions which are tangential to our main concerns and on which we have consistently failed to achieve any agreement.[40]

Perhaps the most significant result of the restriction amendment was the long-awaited approval of VVA's charter by the United States Senate on April 11, 1986. The charter, which had passed the House of Representatives in 1984, officially established VVA as "the only federally recognized veterans' organization aimed specifically at the needs and problems of

American servicemen and women from the Vietnam generation."[41] The charter also authorized the establishment by the VVA of government-sponsored regional outreach offices in VA facilities nationwide.

The VVA charter had been held up in the Senate Judiciary Committee by Senators John East (R-North Carolina), Strom Thurmond (R-South Carolina), and Jeremiah Denton (R-Alabama). Denton opposed VVA's outreach to veterans with less than honorable discharges and the "political action" of some of the VVA leadership. Denton's opposition was critical, because the former POW could legitimately presume to speak for the sentiments of many Vietnam veterans. Denton explained that he had had "serious reservations" about the VVA's history, orientation, and leadership. He objected to recognition because of the organization's "admitting to membership dishonorably discharged veterans and deserters, visits to communist countries of Cambodia and Vietnam, [and] Bob Muller's visit to North Vietnam." A series of meetings between Muller and Denton apparently led to a compromise between the two, with Muller promoting the restriction amendment and moderating his public statements as spokesman for the VVA in exchange for Denton's endorsement of the charter in the Judiciary committee.[42]

Despite the compromise agreement, VVA delegations to Vietnam and Kampuchea are scheduled to continue, mainly to promote American recognition of the government of Vietnam in order to facilitate conclusive results on the Agent Orange/dioxin issue. Only experiments conducted in the "natural laboratory" of the Vietnamese countryside, said Jim Rogers, could lead to those results. In referring to the assimilation of the United Vietnam Veterans Organization into VVA, Rogers declared:

> There's only gonna' be one national organization for Vietnam veterans. The race is already over. In terms of preparing the consciousness of the American people, and consciousness of the Vietnam veteran segment of the American people for some kind of improvement of relations with Vietnam, what VVA [did] was extremely important.[43]

Increased funding for the Agent Orange Testing program in the state of West Virginia has been a priority issue for the State Council's legislative agenda. As of spring, 1986, only two hundred of the approximately 4500 West Virginia Vietnam veterans who had requested testing had been tested. A mortality study conducted by the West Virginia Department of Health compared causes of death for in-country Vietnam veterans, non-combat area Vietnam veterans, and non veterans during the period 1968-1978. While inconclusive, the study lent support to others which suggested that exposure to dioxin in Agent Orange was associated with the development of cancer. The study concluded that ". . . among cancer deaths . . . there was strong statistical evidence to suggest that Hodgkin's disease, cancer of the testis, and soft tissue tumors were more common among veterans who served in Vietnam than among veterans who did not."[44]

Vietnam Veterans of America and the Veterans Administration have clashed regularly over the Agent Orange issue. The VA's record on Agent Orange was so bad, said Robert Muller, that it "defied belief . . . . Nobody could be that insensitive." Author Fred Wilcox, in *Waiting For An Army To Die: The Tragedy Of Agent Orange*, excoriated the VA for its performance on Agent Orange. By 1978, wrote Wilcox, as articles about the possible effects of Agent Orange surfaced nationwide, the VA began to develop a strategy for handling veterans' complaints, which included chronic skin rashes, fatigue, respiratory problems, impaired hearing and vision, depression, and loss of libido. Research done by French scientists in the south of Vietnam suggested that dioxin in Agent Orange caused similar symptoms in Vietnamese who had been exposed, as well as increases in stillborn and deformed infants.[45]

Ironically, VA director Max Cleland, a disabled Vietnam veteran, set a confrontational tone when he instructed the VA to deny all claims for service connected disabilities from Agent Orange exposure, stating that it might be years before scientists could determine whether or to what degree dioxin adversely affected human health. A 1978 memo circulated to all 172 VA hospitals and 58 regional offices declared that herbicides used in Vietnam "have a low level of toxicity . . . . Humans exposed repeatedly . . . may experience temporary and fully reversible neurological symptoms; however, the only chronic condition definitely associated with such exposure is chloracne." Shocked at Cleland's pronouncement, Vietnam veterans and their families were further dismayed by the 1984 class action settlement reached between the producers of Agent Orange and lawyers representing claimant veterans. The settlement was practically universally condemned as inadequate, even scandalous, in the Vietnam veterans community.[46]

The VA persisted in its affirmation that chloracne was the only definite health problem caused by dioxin when proposing regulations for implementation of the 1984 Veterans Dioxin and

Radiation Exposure Act. Charleston surgeon Jim Rogers rebutted the VA's claim in a strongly worded article in *The Guardian*. Rogers cited evidence from a 1984 study released by the Center For Disease Control regarding birth defects among the children of Vietnam veterans in the Atlanta area. The study concluded "several specific types of birth defects were found to be associated with service in Vietnam or the father's exposure to defoliants." Rogers also depended on a Massachusetts mortality study which found a 900% increase among Vietnam veterans of death from soft tissue sarcoma, a rare form of cancer. American chemical workers and Swedish agricultural and forestry workers exposed to Agent Orange also have suffered drastic increases in soft tissue sarcoma.[47]

With tissue samples secured on one of the delegations to Vietnam, said Rogers, VVA conducted its own study which found "no detectable dioxin" in North Vietnamese patients; Agent Orange was not used during the intensive bombing of the North in the latter stages of the war. In South Vietnamese patients, however, "we found the highest average level of dioxin in the world—300% to 400% greater than that of exposed people in North America." There was compelling evidence, he concluded, that dioxin caused specific types of cancer and some birth defects. He recommended that the VA not continue to refuse disability payments to veterans exposed to dioxin during military service. ". . . [S]ome were [injured]," he wrote, "and deserve compensation and treatment for themselves and their children."[48]

"Waiting for an army to die," unfortunately, appeared to be an appropriate title for Fred Wilcox's study of the frustrations endured by Vietnam veterans who suspected that at least some of their physical and emotional difficulties were related to Agent Orange exposure. As time passes, claimants who have received no satisfaction working through the VA bureaucracy are less likely to sustain the energy to pursue their claims. Without systematic and time-consuming testing in the only real laboratory of the effects of Agent Orange, i.e., the Vietnamese countryside, comprehensive results are impossible. Without official recognition by the United States of the government of Vietnam, and normalization of diplomatic relations, those results will not be forthcoming. Positive results from such testing could be economically disastrous for those American chemical companies which produced dioxin for Agent Orange. The string of bankruptcy proceedings could tie up any compensation for years, perhaps decades, and those deserving reparations would likely be beyond help. Proving adverse affects on generations once or twice removed from Vietnam veterans would be difficult. One might conclude from the history of the Agent Orange controversy that the government, the VA, and the chemical industry were, indeed, nervously waiting for an army to die.

Many West Virginia Vietnam veterans, discouraged by their relationship with the VA and the inconclusiveness of Agent Orange testing, perceived the Agent Orange debacle as one of the more extreme examples of the legacy of neglect they have suffered. It was simply further evidence, they reasoned, of their role as the ultimate disposable commodity. "What you got to remember," said one, an ex-Marine, "is that as far as the government's concerned, the Marines are expendable. It means nothing to those people when Marines die. They are no more . . . than a beer can you toss out your window on the interstate. You're expendable. You're no more than a tool."[49]

# Notes, Chapter V

[1]Figley and Leventman, *Strangers At Home*, p. xxviii.

[2]Ibid., p. xxix.

[3]Ibid., p. xxx.

[4]*Washington Post*, February 10, 1978.

[5]Letter, Terry Radke to editor, *Penthouse* magazine, re. article by James Ridgeway, February, 1984. Personal letter, Terry Radke to David Addlestone, April 26, 1984.

[6]A. D. Horne, ed., *The Wounded Generation: America After Vietnam* (Englewood Cliffs, New Jersey: Prentice-Hall, Inc., a *Washington Post* book), pp. 98-99.

[7]*Washington Post*, February 10, 1978.

[8]Interview with Robert O. Muller, Washington, D. C., August 8, 1985. Horne, *The Wounded Generation*, p. 118.

[9]Muller interview.

[10]Ibid.; Interview with David Addlestone, Washington, D. C., August 8, 1985. Conversation with Mike Kaegle, September 12, 1984.

[11]Muller interview.

[12]David M. Bonior, Steven M. Champlin, Timothy S. Kolly, *The Vietnam Veteran: A History of Neglect* (New York: Praeger, 1984), p. 111. Charleston *Gazette*, October 21, 1983.

[13] *The Constitution of the Vietnam Veterans of America, Inc.*, Adopted at National Convention in Washington, D. C., November 9, 1983. Resolutions on Government Affairs, 2nd Vietnam Veterans of America Convetion, Detroit, 1985.

[14]*Washington Post*, February 10, 1978.

[15]Charleston *Daily Mail*, July 13, 1984.

[16]Charleston *Daily Mail*, December 29, 1981. Interview with

Dr. Jim Rogers, Charleston, West Virginia, February 7, 1986. Addlestone interview.

[17]Charleston *Daily Mail*, July 13, 1984.

[18]Charleston Sunday *Gazette-Mail*, July 15, 1984.

[19]Louis Harris/*Washington Post* poll, April 11, 1985, p. 29. Muller interview.

[20]Charleston *Daily Mail*, July 13, 1984. Addlestone interview.

[21]Rogers interview.

[22]Interview with James Hill, Charleston, West Virginia, September 27, 1984.

[23]"Upon written petition by at least three (3) Chapters from within a state, duly organized as hereinafter set forth, or by two hundred (200) individual members from within a state in which less than three (3) chapters have been organized, the President may authorize the formation of a State Council of the Chapters within the petitioning state." Article II, Section I of Constitution of the Vietnam Veterans of America.

[24]Interview with Dave Evans, Charleston, West Virginia, November 10, 1984. Interview with Rich Richards, Charleston, West Virginia, November 10, 1984.

[25]Ibid.

[26]Ibid.

[27]Letter, Robert Muller to David Evans, August 16, 1983. Charleston *Gazette*, November 22, 1983.

[28]Charleston *Gazette*, November 22, 1983. Press release from West Virginia State Council, October 23, 1983.

[29]Evans interview.

[30]*New York Times*, December 12, 1983. Resolutions, Governmental Affairs Committee, VVA, 1st National Convention.

[31]*Washington Post*, November 11, 1983.

[32]Richards interview.

[33]Charleston Sunday *Gazette-Mail*, November 11, 1984. Evans interview.

[34]Constitution of VVA, as amended at 2nd National Convention, November 24, 1985.

[35]Resolutions G-9, G-10, G-11 VVA Governmental Affairs Committee.

[36]Muller interview. Addlestone interview.

[37]Rogers interview.

[38]Interview with Ernestine Thornton, Charleston, West Virginia, February 7, 1986.

[39]Rogers interview.

[40]*The Guardian*, newsletter of Chapter #38, January, 1986.

[41]Duncan Spencer in *The Veteran*, the VVA newspaper, April, 1986, p. 11.

[42]Ibid., p. 11. Robert Muller stepped down as Executive Director of VVA in 1987, and was succeeded by former Army nurse Mary Stout. Muller became administrator of the VVA Foundation.

[43]Rogers interview.

[44]*The Guardian*, February, 1986.

[45]Fred A. Wilcox, *Waiting For An Army To Die: The Tragedy of Agent Orange* (New York: Random House, 1983), pp. 79-80.

[46]Ibid., p. 82. Rogers interview.

[47]*The Guardian*, July, 1985.

[48]Ibid.

[49]Robert Muller, public address at Marshall University, April 21, 1986. Sumrok, Giles, Mitchell-Bateman, *Public Health Legacies*, p. 206. Evans interview.

# Education and Nationalism: The War and West Virginia Vietnam Veterans in the 1980s

The military experience and subsequent civilian homecoming contributed to a significant degree of politicization in some Vietnam veterans, a process Vietnam Veterans of America hoped to direct into a positive Vietnam veterans political movement. The consensual nature of American politics mandated political accommodations in order for VVA to secure recognition from the federal government as the organizational voice of Vietnam veterans. Political compromise has led, as stated earlier, to a curtailment of VVA activism as the organization has increasingly become more strictly a veterans service organization. The agenda of the West Virginia State Council is indicative of VVA's metamorphosis from conscientious political activity to a narrower focus on veterans' benefit issues. Ernestine Thornton ascribed this movement to maturation. Others have attributed it to a nationwide political shift to the right by the American people. Many activist Vietnam veterans, longing to be successfully incorporated into mainstream society, have participated in this shift.

Fred Milano documented political formulation among Vietnam veterans in an article entitled "The Politicization of the 'Deer Hunters:' Power and Authority Perspectives of the Vietnam Veterans." In terms of a stratification or hierarchy of human experiences, the military "is likely to have a great impact on the individual consciousness." Milano found that for youths who have not been separated from their community for any appreciable length of time, military service might provide the initial and perhaps most significant contact with an institution outside the family. Politicization, or the "pronounced restructuring" of one's outlook as a result of dramatic circumstances, could understandably accelerate in such an extreme situation as combat in Vietnam.[1]

The stratified structure of the military, said Milano, may have directed working-class servicemen toward increased class identity within and outside the armed forces, an identification perhaps not realized in the relatively homogenous home communities of most Vietnam veterans. The Vietnam veterans' military experience, combined with a "prolonged process of politicization" brought about by returning to a weak economy and a hostile or indifferent public, created an enhanced political awareness in many of the returnees.[2] The early negative media portrayal of Vietnam veterans stimulated many of them to public activity in order to counteract that image. Ironically, the public image of Vietnam Veterans Against the War, the "counter-culture" profile so attractive to reporters, contributed to the negative image of Vietnam veterans as explosive guerrilla fighters at war with their own society.[3]

Political awareness may have increased in West Virginia Vietnam veterans when they left home, but this has not been reflected in widespread organizational participation. VVA West Virginia State Council president Ernestine Thornton affirmed that many of those who could most benefit from the advocacy of an organization like VVA have not come forward. She attributed this reluctance to Appalachian cultural traits of stoic individualism and independence, reinforced by a deep mistrust of organizational authority due to the veterans' experiences in Vietnam. To West Virginia veterans, she said, family, neighborhood, and hollow were the most important things. She has found little allegiance to statewide organizations. Of some 30,000 Vietnam veterans in West Virginia the older veterans organizations and VVA could account for only 3,000 to 4,000 within their membership, including those veterans with dual memberships. Thornton expected more to join veteran and civic organizations with advanced age, particularly as they were more actively courted by such groups. The VFW, for example, "is out for Vietnam vets [now]. The average age of a World War II veteran is in the late 60s," and VFW needed younger veterans for their dues and active participation.[4]

The political formulation of those Vietnam veterans who had become "politicized" ranged from a radical critique of the war and American society to support for "the national resurgence of artificial patriotism which requires us to go out and kick ass in some other countries."[5] Thornton attempted to explain the position of Vietnam veterans within the patriotic resurgence of the 1980s, which has often glorified the Vietnam war and its veterans:

> This macho image is part of this nationalist movement that we're seeing in the United States . . . that we're all heroes. And we so desperately needed to be heroes. After the Vietnam war and those "lost years," we so desperately needed some heroes. The fact that they are exaggerated may be just the other side of the pendulum. We swung all the way to what shits we were, what a poor generation of soldiers, how terrible our performance was

in Vietnam; we came out of that badly scarred, all of us. You can't be called names forever without feeling it, and carrying some of that with you.

Thornton saw a down side, however, to the new heroic image of Vietnam veterans, sensing a different type of media exploitation, and, more disturbing to her, an effort to "dress up" military adventurism:

> It pisses me off that they're allowed to [commercialize] the Vietnam vet. Sylvester Stallone is laughin' all the way to the bank; the man was a draft dodger. During the Vietnam war he set out [sic] a lot of his time in Switzerland. I think the guy has just ripped off the whole [idea] of Vietnam vets . . .[6]

Several veterans expressed resentment at the artificiality of the "Grade B" movie image of the heroic Vietnam veteran. They were suspicious and cynical about being neglected for years, then suddenly being treated as heroes. The "Rambo mystique" was degrading to Vietnam veterans, said one, in the sense that a solitary warrior returned to the Vietnam jungles to accomplish what American combat soldiers were unable to do, defeat the enemy and liberate prisoners of war. Rambo's victims, noted a Charleston veteran, died "without a mess." Death in combat, he said, "is not clean, it's sickening. When you stab somebody in the chest, everything comes out."[7]

The possibility that draft-age men and women might face a Vietnam-like situation in Central America troubled many Appalachian Vietnam veterans, including Cabin Creek native Dave Evans:

> I was in the first grade when [America's involvement in] Vietnam started. I see kids walking to school today and I wonder if they'll end up in Nicaragua. The kids don't know anything about what happened in Vietnam. They think that going to war is just a macho thing to do. But they've never seen people being pulled out of rice paddies in body bags.[8]

Doug Johnson and others concurred with Evans:

> "Rambo" and all these stupid movies. They keep wantin' to go back and clean it up. You can always tell when we're havin' problems in our country. They start

makin' movies to wave the red, white, and blue. And
what it does is start suckin' these little kids. They say,
"That's what it's all about." I was raised on John Wayne.
That's what I thought it was all about, too. But I found
out a hell of a lot different. And I don't want to see that
happen.[9]

Ernestine Thornton summarized the sentiments of many
veterans who felt they had been used and were determined that a
new generation avoid their plight. She was concerned for the
boys growing up in her family and their possible involvement in
a future war. "It better be a different kind of war," she said. "If
not I've got the money and the gas to get 'em out of the
country."[10]
Although public school students have expressed interest in
the Vietnam era, the educational system in West Virginia has not
adequately met the challenge of sorting out the passions of the
era into a coherent program for study. Not only have many
teachers not reconciled the period in their own minds, but
Vietnam, as recent history, often receives little attention at the
end of the school year. "It's true that teachers do not deal with it
in very much depth," said a Kanawha County administrator.
"There are only so many pages about it in the texts and so much
space in the school year for each historical event." A teacher
reported that "many times classes don't get as far as the Vietnam
War in the course. It comes at the end of the year." Some
teachers have avoided critical analysis of the war as much too
difficult to present fairly. "It's still too controversial an issue to
set up classroom debates about," said one. "I'm concerned with
teaching loyalty and patriotism . . . . If I taught Vietnam, it
would have a pro-American slant. [However] I, myself, am not
really sure about all the issues."[11]
Although the teacher just quoted taught in a city school, his
comments revealed a telling circumstance about public education
throughout the Appalachian region. Social studies professor
Mahlon Brown of Marshall University attributed the avoidance
of critical study of Vietnam to a weakness in the system of
teaching itself. "I don't see the college education system as
equipping teachers to do deep analytical thinking about the
historical process in general," said Brown. He referred to the
"instantaneous society," particulary dependence on movies and
television for shaping attitudes, as "an insidious danger [creating]
a very real problem as to what is reality and what is make
believe. I'm not certain kids coming through now can make that
kind of distinction." The Chair of the Marshall history

department in 1981 expressed his concern that teachers keep the Vietnam War in historical perspective, "in line with all the other wars," if they covered it at all. "In fifty years," he said, "Vietnam may not be all that important."[12]

The inadequacy of public education in West Virginia can be seen primarily as a byproduct of the state's heritage of deprivation. The historical failure of public schools to educate, especially in the poor and isolated areas of the state which have been a fertile breeding ground for soldiers, is perhaps the most tragic legacy of the process of internal colonialism. Poverty, economic exploitation, and local political power struggles have left poor school systems throughout Appalachia generations behind more affluent regions of the United States. Traditionally low in sending high school graduates on to institutions of higher education, and high in the percentage of school dropouts, public schools in the West Virginia hills developed less as a means to remedy the social ills of poverty than as a means to perpetuate them.[13]

As stated earlier, absentee entrepreneurs depend on native allies to enforce the laws and customs which undergird the structure of internal colonialism. The result of power struggles within the ranks of "native colonizers" is a social mechanism physically and culturally removed from outside influence aside from that of the absentee power brokers. The political structure in such a system develops along lines of nepotism and class association among the indigenous colonizers. One powerful component of the mechanism is the office of the local school superintendent, a position from which one can build a political dynasty rooted in the authority to control jobs within the school system and other county offices. The local elites hold the nominal power to effect changes in the system but generally strive to maintain the status quo. Their interest in consolidating their personal position fosters educational programs designed to inhibit questioning, curiosity, and initiative, and to reinforce existing power relationships. Each generation inherits the ideas and attitudes of those which preceded it, denied the motivation and resources to surpass the personal growth and educational standards characteristic of the community.[14]

Community standards in rural Appalachia have often included dropping out of school. During the Vietnam era, some West Virginia counties experienced a high school dropout rate of over 70%. Whatever reasons young West Virginia men had for leaving school, the dynamics of the Vietnam war were in place to channel them into combat. For example, in 1966 the Department of Defense initiated "Project 100,000" to open up the armed service to young men who did not meet normal enlistment standards. New guidelines were drawn up especially to permit the induction of 100,000 underprivileged men annually who would not have qualified under previous mental or physical requirements. "Project 100,000" was supposed to teach skills which the recruits would not learn as dropouts or in their community schools, plus entitle them to veterans benefits upon termination of service. Participants in the project were disproportionately sent to combat. The plan served to avoid the political fallout which might have resulted from a suspension of student deferments or the mobilization of reserve forces. Secretary of Defense Robert McNamara called "Project 100,000" recruits the "subterranean poor." Others called them the "moron corps."[15]

Based on the results of a 1985 newspaper poll, it appears that West Virginia school children have not been exposed to the complexities of the Vietnam experience. The Huntington, West Virginia, *Herald-Dispatch* published the results of a poll containing questions regarding local perceptions about Vietnam. The results showed that area respondents believed that the United States was correct to send the nation's young men to fight in Vietnam. However, only one age group questioned in the poll believed that a future limited war would enjoy popular support. That expression of support came from 18 and 19 year-old respondents, who were in the second and third grades when Saigon fell in 1975.[16]

The sentiments of Huntington area students implied that they had been influenced by the resurgence of pro-military patriotism characteristic of the charismatic leadership of Ronald Reagan, the President with whom they had grown up. When the Vietnam Veterans Memorial was dedicated in Washington, D. C., in November, 1982, the culmination of week-long ceremonies was the recitation of the names of the more than 58,000 American military personnel who died in Vietnam. As their names were being read in the National Cathedral, President Reagan declared that he believed "the names that are being read are of men who died for freedom just as surely as any man who ever fought for this country." Columnist Tom Wicker differed with the president. That the dead from Vietnam died honorably was not in question, he wrote. But if what President Reagan said were really so, the week-long memorial would not have had the "special poignancy" which set it apart from other such occasions. America had been torn apart by Vietnam, said Wicker, precisely because what President Reagan believed was *not* true. Three presidents had been unable to persuade Americans that freedom was at issue in

Indochina to a degree requiring the destructive American intervention which put 58,000 names on the memorial wall. Vietnam, said Wicker, was not a war to end wars or to save freedom, "or to make the world safe for democracy. It was a war entered into for dubious policy reasons, defended on disputed, sometimes false grounds, [and] prosecuted beyond hope of useful results." The memory and sacrifice of those 58,000 Americans, wrote Wicker, should not be blasphemed by any further pretense about the cause.[17]

Tom Wicker was one of many analysts of America in the early 1980s who perceived a willingness to forget or revise the painful lessons of Vietnam. Historian Walter Capps warned of the revival of militarism, a common expectation of impending battle, and "interdependent commitments to strong conservative religion and to a strong national defense." The melding of patriotic zeal with religious fervor was testimony that to many Americans the Vietnam War was "unfinished," and they found it impossible to accept the war's ambivalent preliminary outcome.[18]

Proponents of 1980s religious nationalism concluded that the lessons of Vietnam pointed to a deficiency of national resolve, symptomatic of widespread moral decay. The "first phase" of the Vietnam experience, the war until 1973, failed because American resolve was undermined by the confrontation between heretical "secular humanism" and the country's true destiny as the moral and spiritual beacon of the world. The fundamentalist interpretation of Vietnam was rooted in the concept of Armageddon, wherein the world's fate is determined in a struggle between two opposing and irreconcilable power centers. The politics of Armageddon, or national assertion, wrote Walter Capps, vie for the American mind with the politics of Eden, defined as social democracy and compassionate reform. Both have been present in the American conscience for generations, and Vietnam projected the fundamental quarrel onto the battlefield. Vietnam became a conflict wherein America struggled with America, a conflict that did not end with the suspension of the fighting on the battlefield.[19]

By the time President Reagan declared to the 1981 graduating class at the United States Military Academy that America's "era of self-doubt is over," the preconditions for the embodiment of another Armageddon versus Eden conflict had returned. President Reagan himself foretold the struggle when he declared "I have long believed there was a divine plan that placed this land here  to be found by a people of a special kind, that we have a rendezvous with destiny."[20]

It is uncertain whether Vietnam veterans will play an

organizational role in directing American foreign policy away from future military intervention. Robert Muller was distressed to discover that Vietnam veterans, more so than the American public, declared that they had a clear and definite idea as to their purposes in Vietnam. Ernestine Thornton concurred, estimating that 50-60% of those Vietnam veterans of her acquaintance *would return* to Vietnam if ordered to do so, in spite of their mistrust of authority. The figures cited by Muller and Thornton imply a significant political disharmony among Vietnam veterans, serious enough, probably, to preclude Vietnam Veterans of America from reclaiming a role as an effective political force. Ironically, Muller has concluded that "rather than see this thing [VVA] become a monster, it being another right-wing conservative element, I'd just as soon have it be politically neutral, limit itself to veterans' benefit issues, and stay out of the ballpark of the larger issues."[21]

Many Vietnam veterans, said Muller, who were vocal critics of the war in the late 1960s and early 1970s, when recollections of the pain of the conflict were fresh in their minds, have become distanced from many of those recollections. "With the passage of time, [some of the veterans] tend to forget a lot of the bad stuff, and try to make it a little bit more comfortable by tryin' to think about some of the good stuff." A majority of those who fought in Vietnam were from small towns and rural areas. For veterans to return to a closely-knit community and challenge the fabric of the society which sent them to fight, and particularly to sustain that challenge as they grew older, was a difficult thing to do. "Fighting the war was the biggest, most significant experience of their lives," said Muller. "It's natural that these guys want to feel better about it, so I think they in different ways rationalize it."[22]

The nationalistic movement of America in the 1980s, with the attendant revision of Vietnam into a noble cause, has neutralized or silenced many of the criticisms Vietnam veterans have publicly expressed in the past about the war. Many Vietnam veterans are understandably vulnerable to the heroic rhetoric which has come from the Reagan administration about Vietnam. As Muller concluded "they want to feel better about the experience. If they can look upon themselves as having done the righteous thing and being heroes, they want it. So, they go with the drift of the country, the passage of time."[23]

As some Vietnam veterans have struggled to rationalize their participation in that incomprehensible war, some Americans who avoided service in Vietnam have endured emotional challenges in the wake of the romanticization of the warrior/citizen. Many young men who escaped the draft by virtue of class, status, or a high lottery number, and who may have vilified returning Vietnam veterans, have experienced self-doubt and guilt over their Vietnam era actions as some of the bitterness of the time has receded. Some now endorse the idea of military adventurism for a new generation. Poet Michael Blumenthal, who avoided the draft, concluded that he came up deficient when measured against combat veterans. He declared that the soldiers had intangible strength that he and others like him lacked. "It can be embraced under several headings: realism, discipline, masculinity, resilience, tenacity, resourcefulness. I'm not at all sure they didn't turn out to be better men, in the best sense of the word." Blumenthal reasoned that his avoidance of Vietnam deprived him of a natural rite of passage into manhood. When asked why he did not go ahead and enlist then [in 1983, at age thirty-three], Blumenthal responded that "it would have to have been at that young age, that rite of passage."[24]

Blumenthal's comments seem to confuse two issues. It was one thing to experience guilt about sending another class to fight in one's place, but another to romanticize war itself. Myra MacPherson feared that influential and articulate people such as Blumenthal were grist for the mill of 1980s muscular Americanism. "The more hawkish elements in power," she wrote, "seem to be trying to convince enough people that a win somewhere would erase the shame of Vietnam."[25]

While repentant draft evaders like Blumenthal may serve the purposes of militant nationalism, those Vietnam veterans who maintain an antiwar profile could be an embarrassment to any government which seeks to re-establish American credibility by displays of military strength. As Vietnam veterans become distanced from the war, however, a number of factors can be expected to contribute to their decreased public visibility. Corporate America, for instance, discourages strong loyalty to any subculture which might divert one's energy from the demands of the marketplace, so veterans successfully assimilated into the economic mainstream are likely to minimize their identity as veterans. Those unable or unwilling to assimilate have generally met frustration in their dealings with the government and the public, and as time passes may be expected to withdraw from active advocacy for themselves or other veterans. In all likelihood, a small minority will maintain a level of activism for veterans' rights, and a smaller minority will probably combine this advocacy with political activity and education motivated by a desire to avoid the mistakes which could lead to another Vietnam. One such veteran is Dave Evans, who speaks to students and civic organizations about the lessons of Vietnam, and provides medical care to victims of war in Central America. Another is Doug Johnson. "I'd like to think this country has learned something," said Johnson, "so it doesn't produce another generation of that. We can't afford it. It costs too much."[26]

# Notes, Chapter VI

[1]Fred Milano, "The Politicization of the 'Deer Hunters:' Power and Authority Perspectives of the Vietnam Veterans," in Charles R. Figley and Seymour Leventman, *Strangers At Home: Vietnam Veterans Since The War* (New York: Praeger, 1980), p. 231.

[2]Ibid., p. 231.

[3]Ibid., p. 234

[4]Daniel Sumrok, Steven L. Giles, and Mildred Mitchell-Bateman, "Public Health Legacy of the Vietnam War: Post Traumatic Stress Disorder and Implications for West Virginians," *The West Virginia Medical Journal* 79 (September, 1983): 194. Interview with Ernestine Thornton, Charleston, West Virginia, February 7, 1986.

[5]Interview with David Addlestone, Washington, D. C., August 8, 1985.

[6]Thornton interview.

[7]There was an actual American soldier in Vietnam named John Rambo, the appellation of the fictional Sylvester Stallone character. The real John Rambo, a medic who was opposed to the war, was killed in action in 1968. From a broadside issued by the *War Resisters League*, December, 1986. Interview with Larry Dermody, Charlottesville, Virginia, July 8, 1985. The Charleston *Gazette*, November 1, 1984.

[8]Interview with Dave Evans, Charleston, West Virginia, November 10, 1984. Charleston *Gazette*, November 11, 1984.

[9]Interview with Doug Johnson, Huntington, West Virginia, June 4, 1986.

[10]Thornton interview.

[11]Charleston *Daily-Mail*, October 28, 1981. Public address by Robert O. Muller at Marshall University, April 21, 1986.

[12]Robert Maddox, cited in Charleston *Daily-Mail*, October 28, 1981.

<sup></sup>[13]Peter Schrag, *The School and Politics*, in David S. Walls and John B. Stephenson, *Appalachia in the Sixties: Decade of Reawakening* (Lexington: University Press of Kentucky, 1972), p. 221.

[14]Ibid., p. 223.

[15]James Branscome, "The Crisis of Appalachian Youth," in Walls and Stephenson, *Appalachia in the Sixties*, p. 225. Myra MacPherson, *Long Time Passing: Vietnam and the Haunted Generation* (New York: Doubleday and Company, Inc., 1984), pp. 659-60.

[16]Huntington *Herald-Dispatch*, April 30, 1985.

[17] Charleston *Gazette*, November 13, 1982.

[18]Walter Capps, *The Unfinished War: Vietnam and the American Conscience* (Boston: Beacon Press, 1982), p. 116.

[19]Ibid., p. 136.

[20]Ibid., p. 148.

[21]Interview with Robert O. Muller, Washington, D. C., August 8, 1985. Thornton interview. *Washington Post*/CBS Poll, April, 1985, p. 27.

[22]Muller interview. For further discussion about the romanticization of war with distance in time, see David Kennedy, *Over Here: The First World War And American Society* (New York: Oxford University Press, 1980), pp. 178-230.

[23]Muller interview.

[24]MacPherson, *Long Time Passing*, p. 191.

[25]Ibid., pp. 198-201.

[26]Johnson interview.

# It's A Great Place To Start

Doug Johnson's observation points to some important reasons for studying the political structure which led to America's involvement in Vietnam, a war which created a generation of Americans largely alienated from their country and in many ways alienated from themselves. There is evidence that the structure has not changed significantly since the Vietnam era.

How much has the country learned from Vietnam and its veterans? The architects of credibility did not devise their plans only to fit the particulars of intervention in Southeast Asia. American readiness to "oppose any foe" could also have led to military commitments in Angola, the Belgian Congo, the Dominican Republic, Chile, Guatemala, the Philippines, Cuba, or Brazil. As America has fitfully adjusted to the aftermath of Vietnam, the consideration of military solutions to confirm American credibility has begun to receive a fresh hearing on the American political front. Dependence on military action as an early rather than a final foreign policy option seems to be ascendant. To illustrate, as this is written, thousands of United States National Guard troops are preparing for the most extensive military maneuvers ever conducted in Central America, where United States influence is threatened by nationalist movements.

After years of exposure to the consistently belligerent rhetoric and actions of a strongly pro-military administration under President Ronald Reagan, many in the United States Congress appear to be willing to limit their opposition to militaristic policies to the guarantee that American soldiers will not be used in combat. Should American troops be committed to battle, however, history has shown that initial public and congressional support for such action would probably be strong, in spite of pre-intervention opposition on various fronts. There is little evidence to suggest that most of the American public would not rally behind U. S. troops once they came under fire, at least in the early stages of battle.

The failure of Vietnam led American strategists to reassess not the politics but the tactics of war. War by encirclement, starvation, and domestic terror, designed to destroy the will of civilian populations, is currently in vogue at the Pentagon. Such "low intensity warfare," characterized by hit-and-run operations against civilian targets, has been embraced by war planners as a means to avoid a Vietnam-like "quagmire" with massive U. S. troop deployment and air strikes. While Vietnam may have taught many Americans to listen critically to what the government tells them, the government apparently learned from the Vietnam experience not to tell the American people much of anything about the low intensity military conflicts carried out in their name. Strikes against Grenada in 1983 and Libya in 1986 were carefully managed to control press coverage and potential opposition from Congress. Little word about U. S. sponsorship of war in El Salvador reaches the general public. The government may be gambling that the American public will offer little resistance to military operations which keep the number of dead North American heroes at a minimum, and that the mainstream media will not feel compelled to report "peashooter" wars as long as the casualties are foreigners.

The position of the media is critical as a reflection of the nation's political climate and attitudes toward militarism. In the spring of 1985 the American people were bombarded with television, newspaper, and magazine coverage focusing on the tenth anniversary of the fall of Saigon, signifying the end of the long war in Vietnam. For a brief moment, American's veterans of that war were on center stage. For a brief moment, Vietnam veterans had the parade they were denied when they came home in disgrace from America's big mistake.

The hosannas of April, 1985, probably amounted to no more than a guilty press and a guilty public throwing a penance party. The poignant reunions, the pensive visits to the Vietnam veterans memorial in Washington, the prayers, and the tears were genuine responses to an emotional time, but they were only "news" insofar as they served the transitory purposes of a press and a people anxious to cast out the stigma of rejection they helped impose on America's Vietnam soldiers. The splash of publicity may well have been conceived as much to get the Vietnam veterans monkey off America's back as to pay homage to exploited warriors. Such a media display would have been unlikely in 1975 or even 1980, when the American people were appalled at themselves for allowing Vietnam to happen in the first place and uncomfortable about facing the painful consequences. By 1985, when the realities of the Vietnam debacle were being overshadowed by the vigorous rhetoric of nationalism, America was ready for a show.

It is also possible that years of shouldering a substantial portion of official blame for "losing" Vietnam took a toll on the media. As the government had retreated from blaming the warrior in Vietnam for losing the war, it had shifted more and more approbation to the press and the peace movement. When the American people, in the wake of the war and the Nixon Presidency, were relatively outspoken in demanding government accountability, the media were strong advocates in that direction.

Comfortable in the role of popular advocates, the media hungrily fought off attempts at censorship and news management by Nixon and his spokesmen. As attitudes shifted, however, and an enormously popular president, Ronald Reagan, consistently implied that questioning his administration was disloyal, the media withdrew. The saturation coverage of the new patriotism in the spring of 1985, therefore, can be viewed partly as an act of confession by the contrite national media. In effect, it appeared to be a media apology to Vietnam veterans for telling the truth to the American people about the nature of the war, without adequately drawing the distinction between the conflict itself and those who fought it. That apology was long overdue, but however well intentioned, it reflected to some who viewed it a sense of sanctioning the war. Ironically, the long-awaited distinction between war and warrior was not completely realized. So united were Vietnam and its veterans in America's consciousness that it may not yet have been possible to venerate the combatants without rehabilitating the war. To accept the warrior and reject the war, perhaps, required an admission that American foreign policy, and the system which produced it, was fundamentally flawed. In April, 1985, few Americans seemed willing to make that admission.

The history of America as a world power is marked by policies built upon belligerence. Between the end of World War II and the air strikes against Libya in April, 1986, the United States deployed military forces abroad for political impact more than 215 times.[1] The accelerated use or threat of military action is the central element in the continuing American devotion to the containment of communism. Although economic interests have played a role in America's obsession with containment, the motive is more that of ideological imperialism. In Indochina and elsewhere, ideological imperialism has included vigorous U. S. sponsorship of governments rhetorically or actually opposed to Soviet-type economies or anti-Western political formulations. The methods of the "new imperialism" include the direct use of military, political, and economic power to defeat leftist nationalism, along with efforts to seize political control of entire nations. Vietnam was the first great test of the new imperialism, and the first great failure.[2]

Ideological imperialism depends on an uninformed and relatively powerless American public. The American system is unmatched, wrote historian Howard Zinn, in exercising social control through manipulation of the vote, the workplace, the church, the family, the school, and the mass media. No system is "more successful in mollifying opposition with reforms, isolating people from one another, and creating patriotic loyalty."[3] No example more clearly demonstrates the power of the system to segregate Americans who share common interests than the class-bound nature of the draft during the Vietnam conflict. Those who were favored by the draft laws often limited their opposition to the war to their personal situation. Just as America depended on the political naivete of poor West Virginians, for instance, to support the war unquestioningly, the government counted on the draft-exempt to turn their energy and passions inward, to stay in college, and work toward the day when they would assume their role in the system. The draft isolated students from non-students, preventing them from realizing until too late that the war which threatened their generation could not have been waged without their divisiveness and compliance. The recent mythologizing of Vietnam veterans could be an attempt to appease and silence another potentially troublesome class. The structure of American policymaking is essentially the same as in 1964, and when the managers of policy divine a need for military action, they want no embarrassing symbols of the last war cropping up en masse to put a damper on the exercise.

The system is leaning heavily, as always, on patriotic loyalty to attract a new generation of soldiers. Furthermore, in a society where military escalation is officially promoted as the foundation of both a secure world and a prosperous economy, the armed forces are capitalizing on a constrained job market to promote career training in the military. Recruiting advertisements say little about war, but promise young men and women economic enhancement, college scholarships, and self-actualization in return for serving their country. Recruitment begins early. For example, a major component of the dropout prevention project in the public schools in Cabell County, West Virginia, is a junior Reserve Officer Training Corps program.

Recruiters do not mention that a great number of Vietnam veterans, who were offered similar enticements to those held before today's junior high and high school students, remember the service as dehumanizing. They felt like robots, or machines, or tools, or garbage, or cattle, or slaves. Neither do recruiters mention that the jobs one learns in the service are to a great degree one-dimensional. The military necessarily balances its need for skills against the fact that soldiers may die in combat and must be replaced, like flashlight batteries.[4]

Above all, recruiters do not mention that should their recruits be marched into battle, even if they survive, they may never escape the war. The Vietnam war is not over. Vietnam veterans declared repeatedly that the casualties of that war continue to mount. One need only read the obituaries, for instance, to find the most recent victims, those veterans who have recently committed suicide. The war would end, said many veterans, when the last Vietnam veteran died. Ironically, the medical care provided by Ernestine Thornton and her colleagues in Vietnam, in addition to laying the groundwork for complete recovery for some, brought back a significant number of veterans to lives of permanent dependence and disability. Thornton and the others did their best to restore broken men to life, only to have them rejected, ignored, and vilified by a guilty nation and government. Said one wounded West Virginia veteran:

> There were over 300,000 permanently disabled veterans from that war, and those are people that you're still paying for. You still have to pay compensation, you still have to buy legs and eyes, and hearing aids, braces, and colostomy bags. It isn't paid for and good fiscal policy tells you that if something isn't paid for, you don't go and buy another one.[5]

Young West Virginians, with no memory of Vietnam and little honest inquiry into the war in their schools, are often susceptible to the economic and patriotic appeal of military recruiters, just as Ernestine Thornton, Doug Johnson, Dave Evans, and thousands of others were in 1961, 1963, and 1968. It is ironic that when John F. Kennedy compaigned in West Virginia, military contracts figured prominently in his plans for prosperity in the state. It is significant that many of West Virginia's current political leaders also assign military contracts to the forefront of their plans for economic growth. Recent history suggests the possibility that the system of absentee industrial exploitation which created economic peonage in West Virginia has evolved to a broader system, dependent upon national military-industrial exploitation.

To the double oppression endured by practically all Vietnam veterans, that of being used by a government willing to manipulate their patriotic devotion to duty, and that of being neglected by their culture, can be added the extra dimension of those from a traditionally exploited area such as the state of West Virginia. Historically viewed as disposable commodities by an economic system of absentee colonialism, many of the young people of West Virginia were a ready pool of surplus labor for the "meatgrinder" of Vietnam. Most were unaware of the political realities in which they became involved. They were poorly trained for the war in which they fought, trusting of the supposedly idealistic motivations of a government which lied to them, and embittered by the treatment they received from a guilty and misguided public. Those who went to Vietnam, especially those who have been unable to enter the American mainstream, might well ask whether a new generation of veterans will echo the epitaph one West Virginia soldier bestowed on his Vietnam experience. "I had no choice," he said. "I just got caught up in time."[6]

# Notes, Conclusion

[1]Howard Zinn, *A People's History of the United States* (New York: Harper and Row, Inc., 1980), p. 559.

[2]Seymour Melman, *The Permanent War Economy: American Capitalism in Decline* (New York: Simon and Schuster, 1974), pp. 265-67.

[3]Zinn, *A People's History*, p. 571.

[4]Robert A. Seely, "The Great Deception," *Central Committee for Conscientious Objection Newsletter*, November, 1986.

[5]Interview with Dave Evans, Charleston, West Virginia, November 10, 1984.

[6]Charleston *Gazette*, May 11, 1979.

# Bibliography


**Books**

Addlestone, David et. al. *The Viet Vet Survival Guide*, New York: Ballantine, 1984.

__________________________; Hewman, Susan: Gross, Fredric C. *The Rights of Veterans: The Basic ACLU Guide to a Veteran's Rights*. New York: Avon Books, 1978.

Baskir, Lawrence M. and Strauss, William A. *Chance and Circumstance: The Draft, The War and the Vietnam Generation*. New York: Alfred A. Knopf, Inc., 1978.

Bonior, David M., Champlin, Steven M., and Kolly, Timothy S., *The Vietnam Veteran: A History of Neglect*. New York: Praeger, 1984.

Bourne, Peter G. *Men, Stress and Vietnam*. Boston: Little, Brown, 1970.

Capps, Walter H. *Unfinished War: Vietnam and the American Conscience*. Boston: Beacon Press, 1982.

Caputo, Philip. *A Rumor of War*. New York: Holt, Rinehart and Winston, 1977.

Caudill, Harry. *Night Comes to the Cumberlands: A Biography of a Depressed Area*. Boston and Toronto: Little, Brown and Company. An Atlantic Monthly Press Book, 1963.

Coles, Robert. *Migrants, Sharecroppers, Mountaineers: Volume II of Children of Crisis*. Boston and Toronto: Little, Brown and Company. An Atlantic Monthly Press Book, 1967.

*Diagnostic and Statistical Manual. Edition III*. Washington, D. C.: American Psychiatric Association, 1980.

Dickstein, Morris. *Gates of Eden: American Culture in the Sixties*. New York: Basic Books, Inc., 1977.

Eller, Ronald D. *Miners, Millhands, and Mountaineers: Industrialization of the Appalachian South, 1880-1930*. Knoxville: University of Tennessee Press, 1982.

Erikson, Kai. *Everything In Its Path: Destruction of Community in the Buffalo Creek Flood*. New York: Simon and Schuster, 1976.

Figley, Charles R., ed. *Stress Disorders Among Vietnam Veterans: Theory, Research and Treatment*. New York: Brunner/Mazel, 1978.

__________________________ and Leventman, Seymour, eds. *Strangers At Home: Vietnam Veterans Since The War*. New York: Praeger, 1980.

Fitzgerald, Frances. *Fire In The Lake: The Vietnamese And The Americans In Vietnam*. Boston: Little, Brown, 1972.

Gaventa, John. *Power and Powerlessness: Quiescence and Rebellion in an Appalachian Valley*. Urbana, Chicago, and London: University of Illinois Press, 1980.

Goldman, Peter and Fuller, Tony. *Charlie Company: What Vietnam Did To Us*. New York: Morrow, 1983.

Halberstam, David. *The Best And The Brightest*. New York: Random House, 1972.

Helmer, John. *Bringing The War Home: The American Soldier In Vietnam And After*. New York: The Free Press, 1974.

Herr, Michael. *Dispatches*. New York: Alfred A. Knopf, 1977.

Hersh, Seymour. *The Price Of Power: Kissinger In The Nixon White House*. New York: Summit Books, 1983.

Horne, A. E., ed. *The Wounded Generation: America After Vietnam*. Englewood Cliffs, New Jersey: Prentice-Hall, Inc. A *Washington Post* Book, 1981.

Karnow, Stanley. *Vietnam: A History*. New York: Viking Press, 1983.

Klein, Joe. *Payback: Five Marines After Vietnam*. New York: Alfred A. Knopf, Inc., 1984.

Kovic, Ron. *Born On The Fourth Of July*. New York: McGraw-

Hill, 1976.

Lewis, Helen Matthews; Johnson, Linda; and Askins, Don, eds. *Colonialism in Modern America: The Appalachian Case*. Boone, North Carolina: The Appalachian Consortium Press, 1978.

Lifton, Robert Jay. *Home From The War*. New York: Simon and Schuster, 1973.

MacPherson, Myra. *Long Time Passing: Vietnam And The Haunted Generation*. New York: Doubleday and Company, Inc., 1984.

Melman, Seymour. *The Permanent War Economy: American Capitalism in Decline*. New York: Simon and Schuster, 1974.

Memmi, Albert. *The Colonizer and the Colonized*. New York: Orion Press, 1965.

Paredes, Americo, and Stekert, Ellen J. *The Urban Experience and Folk Tradition*. Austin: University of Texas Press, 1971.

Polner, Murray. *No Victory Parades: The Return Of The Vietnam Veteran*. New York: Holt, Rinehart and Winston, 1971.

Powers, Thomas. *The War At Home: Vietnam And The American People*. New York: Grossman Publishers, 1973.

Santoli, Al. *Everything We Had: An Oral History Of The Vietnam War By Thirty-three Soldiers Who Fought It*. New York: Random House, 1981.

Schell, Jonathan. *The Time Of Illusion*. New York: Praeger, 1980.

Shapiro, Henry David. *Appalachia on Our Minds: The Southern Mountains and Mountaineers in the American Conscience*. Chapel Hill: University of North Carolina Press, 1978.

Starr, Paul. *The Discarded Army: Veterans After Vietnam*. New York: Charter House, 1973.

Terry, Wallace. *Bloods: An Oral History Of The Vietnam War By Black Veterans*. New York: Random House, 1984.

Walls, David S., and Stephenson, John B. *Appalachia in the*

*Sixties: Decade of Reawakening.* Lexington: University Press of Kentucky, 1972.

Weller, Jack. *Yesterday's People: Life in Contemporary Appalachia.* Lexington: University Press of Kentucky, 1965.

Wheeler, John. *Touched With Fire: The Future Of The Vietnam Generation.* New York: Watts, 1984.

Williams, John Alexander. *West Virginia: A Bicentennial History.* New York: W. W. Norton & Company, Inc., 1976.

_______________________________ *West Virginia and the Captains of Industry.* Morgantown: West Virginia University Library, 1976.

Wilcox, Fred. *Waiting For An Army To Die: The Tragedy Of Agent Orange.* New York: Random House, 1983.

Woodward, Comer Vann. *Origins of the New South, 1877-1913.* Baton Rouge: Louisiana State University Press, 1951.

Zinn, Howard. *A People's History of the United States.* New York: Harper and Row, 1980.


**Journals, Periodicals, and Articles**

Ball, Richard. "A Poverty Case: The Analgesic Subculture of the Southern Appalachians." *American Sociological Review* (33): December, 1968, pp. 885-95.

Blauner, Robert. "Internal Colonialism and Ghetto Revolt." *Social Problems* (16): Spring 1969, pp. 397-407.

Boros, J. F. "Re-entry: Facilitating Healthy Readjustment in Vietnam Veterans." *Psychiatry* (36): April, 1973, pp. 428-39.

Branscome, James. "The Crisis of Appalachian Youth." In Walls, David S., and Stephenson, John B. *Appalachia in the Sixties: Decade of Reawakening.* Lexington: University Press of Kentucky, 1972, pp. 225-31.

Broyles, William J. "Why Men Love War." *Esquire* November, 1984, pp. 55-65.

Bruning, Fred. "Sanitizing the Vietnam War." *Macleans* (97:9): July 2, 1984, p. 9.

Camacho, Paul. "From War Hero to Criminal: The Negative Privilege of the Vietnam Veteran." In Figley, Charles R. and Leventman, Seymour, eds. *Strangers At Home: Vietnam Veterans Since The War*. New York: Praeger, 1980, pp. 267-77.

Caudill, Harry. "The Corporate Fiefdom: Poverty and the Dole in Appalachia." *Commonweal* (89): January 24, 1969, pp. 523-25.

Egendorf, Arthur. "Vietnam Veteran Rap Groups and Themes of Postwar Life." In Mantell, D. M., ed. "Journal of Social Issues: Soldiers In and After Vietnam" (31): April, 1975, pp. 111-24.

Johnson, Loch. "Scars of War: Alienation and Estrangement Among Wounded Vietnam Veterans." in Figley and Leventman, *Strangers At Home*, pp. 79-86.

Lewis, Helen Matthews. "Fatalism or the Coal Industry?" *Mountain Life and Work* (XLVI): December, 1970, pp. 4-14.

Milano, Fred. "The Politicization of the 'Deer Hunters:' Power and Authority Perspectives of the Vietnam Veterans." In Figley, Charles R., ed., *Stress Disorders Among Vietnam Veterans: Theory, Research and Treatment*. New York: Bruner/Mazel, Publishers, 1978, pp. 229-47.

Moore, Joan W. "Colonialism: The Case of the Mexican-Americans." *Social Problems* (17): Spring 1970, pp. 463-72.

Schrag, Peter. "The School and Politics." In Walls and Stephenson, *Appalachia in the Sixties*, pp. 219-25.

Stekert, Ellen J. "Focus For Conflict: Southern Medical Beliefs in Detroit." In Paredes, Americo and Stekert, Ellen, eds., *The Urban Experience And Folk Tradition*. Austin: University of Texas Press, 1971, pp. 95-127.

Sumrok, Daniel; Giles, Steven; Mitchell-Bateman, Mildred. "Public Health Legacy of the Vietnam War: Post Traumatic Stress Disorder and Implications for Appalachians." *The West Virginia Medical Journal* (79): September, 1983, pp. 191-98.

Smith, Clark. "Oral History as Therapy." In Figley, Charles R.

ed., *Stress Disorders Among Vietnam Veterans*, pp. 9-18.

Williams, John Alexander. "The New Dominion and the Old: Ante-Bellum and Statehood Politics as the Background of West Virginia's 'Bourbon Democracy'." *West Virginia History* (33): 1971-1972, pp. 314-407.

Wilson, John P. "Conflict, Stress and Growth: The Effects of War on Psychosocial Development Among Vietnam Veterans." In Figley and Leventman, *Strangers At Home*, pp. 231-46.


**Newspapers**

The *Charleston Gazette*, 1960, 1973-1986.

The *Charleston Daily-Mail*, 1973-1986.

The *Fairmont Times*, 1960.

The Huntington *Herald-Dispatch*, 1973-1986.

The *Washington Post*, 1978-1985.

*The Veteran*, 1985-1986. [the national newsletter of Vietnam Veterans of America]

*The Guardian: The Official Newsletter of Chapter 38, Vietnam Veterans of America.* Charleston, West Virginia, 1984-1986.

**Theses and Dissertations**

Crews, James McCrae, Jr. *JFK and the Mountaineers: John F. Kennedy's Rhetoric in the 1960 West Virginia Presidential Primary.* Ph. D. dissertation, Florida State University, 1980.

Houston, Craig Alan. *Four West Virginia Newspapers And Their Editorial Response To The Vietnam War, 1963-1968.* Master's thesis, Marshall University, 1985.

Lawrence, Randall G. *Appalachian Metamorphosis: Industrializing Society on the Appalachian Plateau, 1860-1913.* Ph. D. dissertation, Duke University, 1983.

Simon, Richard M. *The Development of Under Development*

*[sic]: The Coal Industry and its Effect on the West Virginia Economy, 1880-1930*. Ph. D. dissertation, University of Pittsburgh, 1978.

Wilson, John P. *Identity, Ideology and Crisis: The Vietnam Veteran In Transition*. Ph. D. dissertation, Cleveland State University, 1976. Reprinted by Disabled American Veterans Press, Cincinnati, Ohio, 1977.


**Pamphlets and Reports**

*Annual Report 1983-1984*. Department of Veterans Affairs, State of West Virginia.

Costello, Mary. *Vietnam Aftermath*. Washington, D. C.: Congressional Quarterly, Inc., January, 1974.

Feldman, Stuart F. "An Examination of the Lobbying Process: Why Unrepresented Groups Like Vietnam Veterans Need a Lobby." The Committee For Public Advocacy, 1976.

Goodwin, Jim. "Continuing Readjustment Problems Among Vietnam Veterans: The Etiology of Combat Related Post Traumatic Stress Disorders." Cincinnati, Ohio: The Disabled American Veterans Press, 1985.

Leepson, Marc. *Vietnam Veterans: Continuing Readjustment*. Washington, D. C.: Congressional Quarterly, Inc. 1977.

_________________________ *Vietnam War Legacy*. Washington, D. C.: Congressional Quarterly, Inc., 1979.

*Report of Congressional Delegation Trip to Southeast Asia, December 6-17, 1984*. Washington, D. C.: Committee on Veterans' Affairs, 1985.

*State and County Veteran Population, March, 1983*. Washington, D. C.: Office of Reports and Statistics, Statistical Policy and Research Services, Research Division.

*State Profiles of the Veteran Population, Statistical Portraits from the 1980 Census*. Washington, D. C.: Office of Information Management and Statistics, Statistical Policy and Research, December, 1984.

*The Disabled American Veterans Legislative Goals for 1985*. Cincinnati, Ohio: Disabled American Veterans Press, 1984.

*What You Should Know About Vietnam*. The Associated Press, 1967.

**Miscellaneous**

American Friends Service Committee position paper on peace education in West Virginia. @ 1984.

Broadside, War Resisters League. December, 1986.

*Coal Government of Appalachia*. Charleston, West Virginia: Student Task Force for Appalachian Research and Defense Fund, 1971.

*Constitution of the Vietnam Veterans of America*. November, 1983.

__________________________________________________________.
As amended, November, 1985.

Hechler, Ken. *West Virginia Memories of President Kennedy*. Published privately by Ken Hechler, 1964.

Letter from Robert O. Muller to author, June 10, 1985.

Letter from Robert O. Muller to author, July 20, 1985.

Letter from David Evans to Vietnam Veterans of America Foundation, February 18, 1985, re. "Conditions and Needs of Children at Ho Chi Minh Restoration Center."

Personal papers, David Evans, Charleston, West Virginia.

Personal papers, Roger Sanford, Huntington, West Virginia.

Public address by Robert O. Muller at Marshall University, April 21, 1986.

Seely, Robert A. "The Great Deception". *Central Committee for Conscientious Objection Newsletter*. November, 1986.

"Vietnam Poll of the General Population." Released by ABC

News and the *Washington Post*, April 11, 1985.

West Virginia State Council of the Vietnam Veterans of America, Agenda for February 21, 1986.

**Interviews**

Roger Sanford, Huntington, West Virginia, September 11, 1984.

Randy Bowles, Huntington, West Virginia, September 12, 1984.

Glen Hager, Huntington, West Virginia, September 14, 1984.

Roger Sanford, Huntington, West Virginia, September 17, 1984.

Maurice Clark, Huntington, West Virginia, September 20, 1984.

Mark Moore, Huntington, West Virginia, September 24, 1984.

James Hill, Charleston, West Virginia, September 27, 1984.

Jim Rogers, Charleston, West Virginia, September 27, 1984.

John Williams, Huntington, West Virginia, October 13, 1984.

Jeff Payne, Hurricane, West Virginia, October 16, 1984.

Roger Sanford, Huntington, West Virginia, October 19, 1984.

David Evans, Charleston, West Virginia, November 10, 1984.

Rick Richards, Charleston, West Virginia, November 10, 1984.

Bill Fox, Huntington, West Virginia, November 17, 1984.

Ernestine Thornton, Charleston, West Virginia, November 21, 1984.

James Jordan, Charlottesville, Virginia, November 23, 1984.

Gralen Hobble, Charlottesville, Virginia, November 23, 1984.

David Evans, Elkview, West Virginia, February 6, 1985.

Harry Beam, Huntington, West Virginia, February 11, 1985.

David Evans, Huntington, West Virginia, February 24, 1985.

Louis Peake, Huntington, West Virginia, March 13, 1985.

David Smythers, Kenova, West Virginia, April 3, 1985.

Al Van Dyke, Charlottesville, Virginia, July 5, 1985.

Larry Dermody, Charlottesville, Virginia, July 8, 1985.

David Addlestone, Washington, D. C., August 8, 1985.

Robert O. Muller, Washington, D. C., August 8, 1985.

Frederick Donovan, Charleston, West Virginia, February 7, 1986.

Jim Rogers, Charleston, West Virginia, February 7, 1986.

Ernestine Thornton, Charleston, West Virginia, February 7, 1986.

Doug Johnson, Huntington, West Virginia, May 15, 1986.

Doug Johnson, Huntington, West Virginia, June 4, 1986.

Perry Campbell, Huntington, West Virginia, June 20, 1986.

# About the Author

John Hennen was born in Huntington, (Cabell County), West Virginia in 1951. Since graduating from college in 1975, he has divided his time between his home state and Virginia, working as a dishwasher, housepainter, apprentice billboard artist, warehouseman, and youth counselor. *Caught up in Time* grew out of interviews he conducted for the Oral History of Appalachia Project at Marshall University, where he earned a master's degree in American history in 1987. In 1986 and 1987, he was associate editor of *West Virginia History*, the state's historical journal, published by the Department of Culture and History in Charleston. Mr. Hennen is currently a doctoral student in Appalachian History and Culture at West Virginia University in Morgantown.